Answers To The
50 Biggest Online Business Mistakes

Fix What's Broken, Skip the Struggle, and Finally Build a Business That Works

Disclaimer

PREFACE

Why We Wrote This Book, and Why You'll Be Glad You Picked It Up

If you're holding this book, chances are you're already running an online business, or you're trying to. And chances are, you've already realized this path isn't quite as simple as the gurus make it sound.

We get it. We've both been there.

Between us, we've worked behind the scenes for hundreds of online businesses, launches, and digital campaigns. We've seen what works. More importantly, we've seen what doesn't.

Years ago, we co-authored The 50 Biggest Website Mistakes, a book that helped thousands of entrepreneurs avoid the costly design and technical pitfalls that were holding their websites back.

But what we realized was... a broken website is just one piece of the puzzle. Even if your website is clean and functional, it won't matter much if your business is built on shaky ground.

That's where this book comes in. We've pulled together the most common, most painful, and most fixable mistakes we've seen online business owners make, whether they're just getting started, pivoting, or trying to scale up.

This isn't theory. These are the real-world missteps that quietly drain your time, your energy, and your income.

And we're not here to judge, we're here to help. Because we've made plenty of these mistakes ourselves.

- We've launched before we were ready.
- We've undercharged.
- We've skipped the boring-but-important stuff.
- We've said, "I'll figure it out later", and paid the price.

What you'll find in the pages ahead isn't fluff, filler, or recycled advice. It's the hard-won, no-nonsense truth about what it really takes to build an online business that actually works.

If you're ready to stop guessing...
If you're tired of spinning your wheels...
If you want to finally build a business that pays off instead of burning you out...

Then turn the page. Let's fix what's broken. Let's simplify what's complicated. And let's get your business moving forward, on purpose.

To your success,
Frank Deardurff III & Bret Ridgway

Table of Contents

Table of Contents

Mindset & Planning Mistakes

Where most businesses go off the rails before they even leave the station.

Before the first sale… before the logo… before the website even goes live, your mindset and your plan shape everything.

This section isn't about flashy tools or clever hacks. It's about the *foundation* your business is built on. Because if your thinking is off, your strategy is fuzzy, or you're chasing trends instead of solving real problems, nothing else you do will stick.

We've both seen far too many entrepreneurs grind for years without traction, all because they skipped the groundwork. Don't make that mistake.

These chapters are here to help you fix what's *under the hood*, so when you hit the gas, your business actually moves.

Chapter 1: Starting Without a Clear Business Plan

Let's cut straight to it, **starting an online business without a plan is like building a house without blueprints.** You might end up with something that sorta looks like a business, but it's probably got leaks, and bad wiring, and nobody's going to want to move in.

You wouldn't hire a contractor who just "wings it," right? So why in the world would you build your business that way?

The Myth of "Just Start"

We get it. There's a lot of talk out there about "just start." And don't get me wrong, we're all for taking action. But there's a massive difference between taking action with *intention* and flailing around in the dark.

We've seen it over and over again. Someone buys a domain, installs WordPress, maybe throws up a logo, and calls it a business. No offer. No customer research. No pricing strategy. No clue where traffic is going to come from.

Then they wonder why nobody's buying.

Starting a business without a plan isn't bold, it's blind.

A Plan Doesn't Mean a 50-Page Document

Let's kill another myth while we're at it. We're not talking about some stuffy, corporate-style plan filled with charts and projections no one will read.

We're talking about a **simple, actionable roadmap** that answers core questions like:

- What problem do I solve?
- Who am I solving it for?
- What am I offering (and how do I deliver it)?
- How will people find me?
- What are my revenue goals, and how will I hit them?
- What tools, systems, and support do I need?
- What's my exit plan, or at least the end goal?

You don't need an MBA. You just need clarity.

Without a Plan You're Building a Hobby, Not a Business

Here's a tough pill: **If you don't have a plan to make money, you don't have a business, you have a project.**

"If You Fail to Plan, You Are Planning to Fail"
- *Benjamin Franklin.*

Too many online entrepreneurs fall into the trap of playing business. They pick colors. They design a slick logo. They buy plugins and tools they don't use. But they've got no structure. No system. No strategy.

And months later? They're burned out, broke, and blaming the algorithm.

But the problem wasn't Instagram. Or SEO. Or the niche.
The problem was the foundation. Or lack of one.

The Freedom Trap

A lot of folks go into online business for freedom, and that's a beautiful thing. Freedom of time. Freedom of income. Freedom to work in your PJs.

But the irony is this: **freedom comes from structure. Not chaos.**

A solid plan creates boundaries. It lets you measure progress. It gives you clarity when things get noisy (and they *will* get noisy). It helps you make decisions faster and more confidently.

Freedom *without* a plan is just spinning your wheels. And you don't get freedom from that, you get frustration.

"But I Don't Know What I Don't Know…"

We hear this all the time. And that's fair. Especially when you're just starting out.

But guess what? That's exactly why you *need* a plan. Because a plan shows you where the gaps are. It forces you to get the info you're missing before you make expensive, painful mistakes.

And if you're really lost? Get help. Find a mentor. Join a group. Invest in training. Ask the right questions. You're not supposed to know everything from day one, but you *are* responsible for building a path to get there.

A Real-World Example

There was someone who once reached out to Frank, let's call him Dan, who was ready to "go big" with his online coaching business. He'd spent months building a gorgeous website. Hired a designer. Paid for the fanciest tools. Even had a podcast ready to launch.

But he never once validated his offer. Didn't know what his audience was struggling with. Had no idea how to drive traffic. His pricing? Pulled out of thin air.

Dan had built a beautiful shell. But there was nothing inside.

We stripped it back. Built a lean plan. Identified his ideal client. Clarified his core offer. Set up a simple funnel. He made more money in 90 days with *less effort*, because we stopped playing business and started building one.

Your Action Step

Don't skip this. If you don't already have a clear business plan, grab a notebook or open a Google Doc and answer these 7 questions right now:

1. Who do I help?
2. What problem do I solve?
3. How do I solve it (what's my offer)?
4. What makes me different?
5. How will I get traffic?
6. How will I convert that traffic?
7. What's my goal in the next 90 days?

That's your starting blueprint. Refine it as you go, but get something in place before you build another landing page or launch another offer.

Bottom line?

A plan doesn't guarantee success. But starting without one all but guarantees failure.

Let's build smarter. Let's build with purpose. Let's build like we mean it.

Chapter 2: Chasing Trends Instead of Solving Real Problems

Let us just shoot straight with you…

Trends? They're like fireworks, flashy, loud, and gone before the smoke clears.

But problems? Oh, they stick around. Like that squeaky cabinet door you keep ignoring.

If you're hitching your business to the latest shiny object, crypto, NFTs, drop shipping, AI doodads, or whatever TikTok's hyping this week, you're not really building a business.

You're just playing digital hopscotch.

Now look, Frank's a tech guy. He *loves* cool tools. He's been in this game long enough to see trends pop up, blow up, and burn out. Some stick. Most don't.

And the folks who get burned the worst? They built their whole business on hype, not on a *need*.

The Classic "Squirrel!" Moment

You know what he's talking about. That itch to dive headfirst into the next big thing.

- You see a guru's screenshot of a $100K payday.
- Your inbox blows up with "You've GOT to try this!" subject lines.
- You start thinking… "Maybe this is *it*. The shortcut I've been waiting for."

But let's hit you with something real:

There are no shortcuts to trust.

It's trust, not trends, that gets people to pull out their wallets. You build a business on solving problems, not chasing whatever's trending this week.

It's the difference between building a shack on sand and laying a foundation on solid rock.

Businesses That Last Solve Problems That Matter

Think about the brands that have been around for a decade or longer. They're not living on hype fumes, they're solving actual problems.

Amazon? Sure, they started with books. But what really made them explode? They made buying easy. They solved the *inconvenience*.

Calendly? It's not sexy. But it crushed the annoying back-and-forth of scheduling. Problem solved.

Even Frank and Bret's businesses? They didn't grow them by jumping on every flashy web trend. Frank helped people fix broken websites, get more leads, and stop losing sales. That's real. That's needed. That *still* matters.

When You Build Your Business Around a Real Pain Point, Everything Clicks

Seriously, when you stop guessing what your audience *might* want and instead zero in on what's keeping them up at night, something magical happens.

You don't have to shout. You don't have to beg. You don't have to play gimmicky games to get attention.

Because people are already searching for a solution.

- They're typing it into Google.
- They're venting about it on social media.
- They're talking to their friends, saying, *"Man, I wish someone could just fix this already."*

That's your cue.

And when you show up with an answer to that *exact* problem? You instantly stand out, not because you're louder, but because you're *relevant*.

You're not another voice in the noise. You're the *relief*.

You become the person who "gets it." You're not selling. You're helping. And people can feel that difference.

Let us tell you, that *trust skyrockets* when your message lines up with someone's struggle.

You speak to what they're feeling. You reflect what they're thinking. It's like you reached into their brain and said, "Hey, I know exactly what you're dealing with... and I've got something that can help."

That kind of alignment? It builds loyalty. It builds referrals. And yeah, let's not ignore the obvious, it lets you **charge more**.

Because when you solve a painful, persistent problem, your offer becomes *valuable*. Not just another option... but *the* solution.

People don't haggle when they're hurting. They just want relief, and they'll gladly pay the person who delivers it with clarity and confidence.

So instead of chasing attention, start chasing *understanding*. Get obsessed with the pain your audience is already feeling.

Once you do? Your messaging gets easier. Your offers land harder. And your business finally starts to grow in the *right* direction.

"But Guys, Trends Make Money..."

Yeah... *sometimes*. For a little while. But let's be honest, most of the people cashing in are the ones selling the course about the trend.

They're handing you pickaxes while they're walking away with the gold.

Here's what we always tell people:

It's one thing to use a trend in your marketing.

It's another to base your whole business on it. One's a tool. The other's a gamble. If you want something sustainable, anchor to *purpose*. Not popularity.

The Quick Filter Test: Trend or Real Problem?

Before you jump into the next big thing, ask yourself:

- Is this just a cool tool, or does it *actually* fix something?
- Is this solving a pain people already know they have?
- If the trend died tomorrow, would anyone still care about this?

If you can't say yes to that last one, you're just chasing a trend.

But if the pain sticks around, **you've got something real to build on**.

Your Turn: Action Time

We want you to pause and think about this:

What's the actual problem you solve?

Not just what you *do*. Not the tool you use. But the actual, frustrating, pull-your-hair-out problem you help people get rid of.

Would people still pay you to solve that five years from now?

If not, how can you dig deeper? What problem's always going to be there that you can anchor your business to?

Write it down. Get clear. Because that right there? That's your compass. That's your direction when the next shiny object rolls in.

Bottom line?

Trends are fun. But fun doesn't build freedom.

Solving problems does.

So don't fall for the hype trap. Stay focused on helping real people fix real pain.

Because while hype fades...

People will *always* pay for solutions.

Chapter 3: Thinking "Build It and They Will Come"

If there's one lie that's crushed more online dreams than bad hosting and shady gurus combined, it's this one:

"Build it and they will come."

No, they won't.

Just because you launched a shiny new website, added your logo, and wrote a blog post… doesn't mean anyone knows you exist.

We hate to break it to you, but there's no magical traffic fairy out there sending people your way just because you hit "publish."

Websites Don't Attract People, Marketing Does

Look, Frank has been helping people build websites for over two decades. And he can't tell you how many folks have come to him after spending weeks (or months) working on their site, only to sit there refreshing their dashboard wondering why the traffic needle isn't moving.

They'll say, "Frank, I launched. I even shared it on Facebook once!"

He'll say, "Great. And then what?"

Crickets.

Launching a website is not the finish line, it's the starting gate.

What comes next is where the real work (and success) begins.

The Field of Dreams Fallacy

That famous line, "If you build it, they will come", worked in a movie because it was backed by Hollywood magic.

But your website isn't sitting in a cornfield with ghost baseball players. It's sitting in a sea of **1.1 billion** other websites. And most of them are gathering dust, just like yours will if you don't have a plan to get people there.

People don't just "show up." You've got to **earn** their attention, and that takes effort, strategy, and consistency.

Just Building a Website is Like Opening a Store in the Desert

Imagine opening a store in the middle of nowhere. You spend weeks decorating, putting up signs inside, getting your products stocked... but you forget one crucial thing:

There are no roads to your store.

That's what a website with no traffic strategy is. It's a beautifully designed ghost town.

If you want people to show up, you need to pave a path. That means:

- Content marketing
- SEO
- Email list building
- Social media outreach
- Paid traffic (done wisely)
- Strategic partnerships
- Lead magnets and funnels
- Being where your audience already hangs out

And even then, you've got to keep showing up. Repetition builds recognition. Visibility builds trust. Trust leads to clicks, and clicks turn into conversions.

You Need a Visibility Plan Before You Launch

We'll be blunt: **If you don't know how you're going to get traffic, you're not ready to launch.**

And we don't mean vague ideas like "social media" or "SEO." We mean specifics.

- What platform will you focus on first?
- What type of content will attract your ideal visitor?
- How will you get that content in front of them?
- What will you offer to get them on your email list?
- What's the first thing you'll ask them to do once they're on your site?

If you can't answer those questions, don't build more pages. Build a traffic strategy.

We've Been There

Early in my career, we made this exact mistake. Each of us built membership sites in separate niches. We had the tech all lined up. Everything looked slick.

We both launched… and then waited.

And waited.

And waited some more.

What we realized was, *we hadn't told anyone about our membership sites in the right way.* We thought people would just find them. We had no outreach plan, no email list, no pre-launch buzz, nothing.

So, what happened?

We had to go back and do things the right way, build relationships, create lead magnets, email the list, run promotions, show up on podcasts... **and that's when they took off.**

Your Action Step

Let's stop pretending traffic is accidental.

Before your next launch, sit down and map out:

1. **Where will your first 1,000 visitors come from?**
2. **How will you consistently bring in new traffic each week?**
3. **What action do you want people to take when they land on your site?**
4. **What can you offer that makes your site worth sharing?**

Remember: traffic doesn't just "happen." It's built. Earned. Engineered.

Bottom line?

You can build the best site in the world. But if no one knows it's there, it might as well not exist.

- Don't just build it, promote it
- Don't just launch it, ignite it
- Don't wait for them to come

Go get them.

Chapter 4: Not Treating It Like a Real Business

Let's have an honest moment here.

One of the biggest mistakes we see, and we've made it ourselves, is this:

Starting a business... and then treating it like a hobby.

You say you're "working on your online business," but your laptop's on the kitchen counter next to an unfinished grocery list. You're "launching soon," but you haven't touched your website in three weeks. You've got offers, but no pricing. Clients, but no process.

And here's the thing...

It doesn't matter if you're just getting started or if you've been in the game a few years, **if you're not treating it like a real business, don't expect real business results.**

It's Easy to Pretend

We get it. We've done it too.

You fiddle with the logo. You update your Instagram bio (again). You buy another domain name you'll never use. You're doing "business-y" stuff, but you're avoiding the real stuff, the stuff that actually makes money, helps people, and moves things forward.

You're busy. You're active. But if we're being honest? You're hiding from the hard parts of running a business.

- Like making decisions
- Setting prices
- Following up with prospects
- Actually asking for the sale
- Getting systems in place that make this thing *work*

When you're not clear on what kind of business you're building, or worse, when you're *afraid* to really go for it, it's tempting to just play business instead.

The Turning Point

Frank remembers when it hit him.

He had a full client load. He was doing work that mattered. But behind the scenes? It was duct tape and good intentions. His "system" was sticky notes, a few emails, and hoping he remembered what he promised someone last week.

Then one of his biggest clients sent him a message:

"Hey, do you have a contract or invoice for this?"

He didn't. He had nothing. Just trust. And even though things were fine with his client, he felt exposed.

That was the moment he realized he did have a *real* business... but he just wasn't acting like it.

No official paperwork. No dedicated bank account. No set office hours. No structure. And as long as he treated it like something casual, it would never become anything more.

You Don't Need an Office, You Need Ownership

Don't get caught thinking a "real business" means a building, a team, and a nameplate on the door.

Real business is about ownership.

- Ownership of your time
- Ownership of your income
- Ownership of your process and how you show up for people

It's about treating your calendar like it matters. It's about getting serious about how you handle money, client relationships, and your future.

If you're waiting until you hit a certain revenue goal before you start acting like a pro, let me tell you... you've got it backwards.

The moment you decide to show up differently, that's when your results start to change.

"Opportunity is missed by most people because it is dressed in overalls and looks like work."

- Thomas Edison

Why It Matters

When you treat your business casually, guess what kind of clients you attract? Casual ones.

The flaky kind. The non-paying kind. The kind who don't respect your boundaries because, well... you don't really have any.

But when you start showing up with professionalism, even in small ways, like sending a clear proposal, having an onboarding process, and keeping your word, people notice.

You create trust. You create authority. You stop being "just another freelancer" and start being *the one* they trust with the big stuff.

That's when your rates go up. That's when referrals start rolling in. That's when your business *feels* like a business.

Your Action Step

Ask yourself, right now, if someone looked at how you're running your business, would they call it professional?

- Do you have set hours?
- A clear way to accept payment?
- A legal business name or entity?
- An actual follow-up process?
- A way to track money in and out?

If the answer is no, or "sort of", that's your cue.

Pick one area to tighten up this week. It doesn't have to be complicated. Just make one part of your business a little more real, a little more stable.

Because the more seriously you take it, the more seriously others will, too.

Bottom line?

You don't grow into a real business by accident. You grow into it by *owning it.*

Not someday. Not when the money's flowing. But now, before it looks like much to anyone else.

Show up like it matters. Because it does.

Chapter 5: Avoiding Investment in Growth Tools or Training

Let me tell you something that might sting a little...

You can't expect your business to grow if you're not willing to grow yourself.

We've had many conversations over the years with entrepreneurs who say they want to "take their business to the next level," but when it comes time to invest in the tools, resources, or training to actually get there? They freeze up tighter than a budget spreadsheet.

Now we get it. We really do. We know what it's like to be cautious with spending, especially when you're starting out or trying to dig out of a slump. You want to be wise with your money, and you should be.

But there's a big difference between **being wise** and **being cheap.**

Being wise is asking, "Will this tool or training help me serve better, sell smarter, or scale faster?"

Being cheap is asking, "Can I just find a free version and figure it out on my own... even if it takes 10x longer and doesn't work as well?"

The problem is, that many people spend *years* trying to DIY their way to success with duct tape strategies, random YouTube videos, and outdated plugins, instead of learning from someone who's already walked the road, or investing in the tools that were literally built to make their life easier.

They end up frustrated, stuck, and overwhelmed… and eventually, many of them quit, not because their idea was bad, but because they didn't equip themselves to carry it forward.

Been There, Done That

Back when Frank first started building websites for others, he was the king of "I'll figure it out myself." Actually, he had to figure it out himself considering he's been online before Google.

But even after that, he spent late nights hacking together bits of code, troubleshooting problems that a $49 plugin could've solved in five minutes, and second-guessing every purchase like it was going to bankrupt him.

He was doing everything the hard way and wearing it like a badge of honor.

But let us tell you… pride doesn't pay the bills. **Speed and skill do.**

Once he finally started investing in the *right* training and tools, everything changed. He wasn't reinventing the wheel, he was learning from people who had already paved the road.

He wasn't wasting time, he was getting more done, in less time, with less stress. And that freed him up to do what he does best: build, teach, and help others win online.

You're Either Spending Time or Money, Pick One

One of the most important lessons we've learned (and taught) over the years is this:

> **You'll always pay. The only question is, will you pay in time, or will you pay in money?**

Trying to "save money" by not buying the right email tool or refusing to pay for a course that walks you through a proven system? That decision can end up *costing you way more* in missed opportunities, frustration, and months of spinning your wheels.

Meanwhile, your competitors are moving faster, converting better, and building smarter, because they've got the right support behind them.

We're not saying you need to go on a spending spree. We're saying: **invest with intention.** Ask yourself what's slowing you down, or what's standing between you and your next level.

Sometimes it's a skill gap. Sometimes it's a tech gap. Either way, the fix usually isn't more hustle, it's better tools, smarter strategies, or a mentor who's already made the mistakes you're about to make.

"But What If It Doesn't Work?"

We hear that one all the time.

And here's what we say: if you're afraid to invest in something that could help you grow, ask yourself what fear is actually behind that.

Is it the fear that it won't work? Or is it the fear that *you won't follow through*?

Because honestly? Most of the time, it's not the tool or the course that fails, it's that we don't *use* them. We buy them, we log in once or twice, then we move on to the next thing without ever digging in.

We've been guilty of that, too. That's why we ask ourselves now, "Am I ready to use this? Are we clear on what we want out of it? Will we commit to applying it?"

If the answer's yes, we buy with confidence. Because we know growth doesn't come free. It comes from making smart, strategic decisions that stretch me forward.

Your Action Step

Take a moment and ask yourself:

Where are you currently stuck in your business? What's been sitting on your to-do list for way too long?

Now ask: what would it take to fix that? Is there a tool that could automate it? A training that could teach you how to do it faster or better? And most importantly: **what's the cost of staying stuck where you are?**

Because here's the truth… Not investing is *still* a choice. And it might be the most expensive one you make.

Bottom line? - You can't grow a business on freebie hacks and guesswork. At some point, you've got to put skin in the game.

Success isn't free, because growth isn't either.

But when you invest in the right tools, training, and mentors, you're not just buying information.
You're buying *momentum.*

And that's priceless.

Chapter 6: Setting Unclear or Unmeasurable Goals

Let us ask you something simple, but important:

If we asked you right now what your goal is for the next 30 days in your business, could you tell us, clearly and confidently?

No vague "I just want to grow" or "I want to make more money" answers. I'm talking specifics. Like:

"I want to get 500 new subscribers by the 30th."
"I want to close 10 new clients at $1,500 each."
"I want to launch my course and make $3,000."

If that kind of clarity feels like a stretch, don't worry, you're not alone. **But that might be exactly why you're stuck.**

Hope is Not a Strategy

Bret says one of the most common traps he sees online business owners fall into is this idea of "just working hard" and trusting it'll all come together.

They're posting on social, writing emails, tweaking landing pages, building products, and then wondering why none of it's producing the results they hoped for.

But the truth is, if you're not aiming at a clear target, how do you know if you're on track, or completely off course?

You can't measure progress toward *vague*. You can't improve what you don't define.

"You can't improve what you don't measure."
- *Peter Drucker*

Why Clarity Creates Momentum

Setting real, measurable goals isn't just about keeping score. It's about focus. It's about direction. It's about knowing where you're heading so you can make better decisions *right now*.

Without goals, every task feels equal. You waste time perfecting graphics that don't matter, fiddling with fonts, or rewatching tutorials you'll never use.

But when you have a goal? Suddenly, things line up:

- You know what needs to be done *this week*.
- You know which tasks move the needle and which ones are distractions.
- You can say "yes" to the right opportunities, and "no" to the shiny ones.

- You get to the end of the month and say, "I made progress," not "Where did the time go?"

Goals give your hustle a purpose. They turn busy work into results.

Frank's Made This Mistake More Than Once

Early in his journey, he was grinding day and night. Building websites. Writing content. Launching tools. And yes, he was making some money, but he was also stuck in a cycle of being "busy," not *productive*.

Why? Because he wasn't setting measurable goals. He'd write things like "Grow the business" or "Launch a new product," and then wonder why he felt frustrated or overwhelmed two months later.

The moment he started attaching real numbers and timelines to my goals, everything shifted.

Now he could track progress. Now he could adjust when things weren't working. Now he had a reason to celebrate a win *and* a system for fixing a miss.

That shift took him from reaction mode to intentional action, and my business grew right alongside it.

Vague Goals = Vague Results

Let's break it down.

"I want to grow my email list" sounds nice…

…but "I want to add 250 subscribers in the next 30 days" gives you a finish line.

"I want to sell more" is a good wish…

…but "I want to close 5 sales at $497 this week" turns it into a target.

The more specific your goal, the more measurable your results. And that's how you improve, by measuring and adjusting, not guessing and hoping.

"But What If I Don't Hit the Goal?"

Good question. And here's the honest answer: **You might not.** And that's okay.

Because the point of a goal isn't perfection, it's *progress.* Even if you fall short, you'll learn more, try more, and grow more than if you didn't set the goal in the first place.

But here's the real danger:

When you don't set a goal at all, you'll never know how close, or how far, you actually are. You'll always feel like you're spinning your wheels.

Setting goals, even ones that stretch you, is how you get out of neutral and start shifting gears.

Your Action Step

Let's make this practical.

Take 10 minutes right now and write down **three measurable goals** for the next 30 days. Something like:

- Launch [your product] and generate $X in revenue
- Grow your email list by [number] subscribers
- Book [number] of discovery calls or demos

Be specific. Set a deadline. Write it where you can see it every day.

Then reverse-engineer the steps to get there. Break it down into weekly actions, then daily actions.

If it helps, share your goal with someone who can keep you accountable, or even post it publicly.

Because once your goal becomes real, your focus will follow.

Bottom line?

You can't hit what you don't aim for. And you can't improve what you're not tracking.

Set clear goals. Measure your results. Adjust as you go.

This isn't just about ambition, it's about *intention.* That's how real businesses grow.

Chapter 7: Ignoring Time Management and Productivity Systems

Let's get one thing straight...

You don't need more hours in the day. You need a better way to use the ones you already have.

One of the most overlooked success killers we see, especially with online business owners, is not having any sort of structure for how they manage their time. No systems. No schedule. No real plan for what their day looks like... just a hope that somehow it'll all get done.

Spoiler alert: it never does.

Busy Doesn't Mean Productive

You ever have one of those days where you're constantly moving, but at the end of it, you think, *"What did I actually accomplish?"* That's what happens when you don't manage your time, you just react to it.

You wake up, check your email, scroll a bit on social, reply to a few messages, maybe fiddle with your website, or try to write a post. But nothing *moves the business forward.*

And it's not because you're lazy. It's because you're working without a map. You're letting the day happen *to* you, instead of taking charge of it.

How Frank Learned the Hard Way

When Frank first went full-time online, he thought the biggest perk was the freedom. No boss. No time clock. No one breathing down my neck.

And for a while, he loved that.

But then the days started blurring together. He'd jump from task to task, work late nights, miss dinner, and still feel behind. He wasn't running his day, his day was running him.

At some point, he had to stop and realize: that **freedom without structure is just chaos with better marketing.**

That's when he started getting serious about managing my time like the asset it is.

You Can't Scale on Randomness

Let us put it another way...

If you're doing everything "when you get to it," you'll never get to it.

Waiting until inspiration strikes, until the house is quiet, or until your inbox is caught up? That's a trap. A productivity black hole.

Systems aren't about being rigid. They're about being intentional.

When you know what you're working on, and when, your brain doesn't have to negotiate with you all day. You don't waste energy deciding what's next. You just get to work.

And when your business starts to grow, and it will if you stick with it, you'll need those systems more than ever. You can't scale "winging it." You scale what's repeatable.

Don't Overcomplicate It

You don't need 17 apps or a color-coded Kanban board to be productive. What you do need is a rhythm that works for *you.*

Maybe it's time blocking your calendar. Maybe it's batching similar tasks on certain days. Maybe it's starting your day with one "needle mover" before you touch anything else.

Whatever it is, **you have to find a system and actually stick to it.**

It's not about being perfect. It's about being consistent.

The more consistent you are with how you manage your time, the more predictable your results become. And predictable results? That's how real businesses grow.

Why Most People Avoid It

Here's the real truth: most people avoid productivity systems because they don't want to face how much time they're wasting.

That was us at one point, too.

When we first started tracking where our time actually went, we both had to swallow some hard truths. A lot of "working" time was actually just *avoiding* the real work, getting lost in busy tasks that made us feel productive, but weren't doing a thing for our income or impact.

But once we saw it for what it was, we could fix it. We could trim the fat. Cut the noise. Get laser-focused.

And the best part? We got our evenings back. We started *finishing* our workdays. We stopped chasing time and started owning it.

Your Action Step

If you've been flying by the seat of your pants, here's what we want you to do today:

Start tracking your time. For the next three days, jot down (honestly) what you're doing each hour. Not just work tasks, everything. Then step back and review it.

Ask:

- Where's the wasted time?
- What could've been batched or delegated?
- What tasks actually moved the business forward?

Once you see it clearly, build a basic system. Just one. Maybe a "first 90 minutes focus window" or a set day for content creation. Whatever it is, start small and build from there.

Because the moment you start *owning* your time… your business starts serving *you*, not the other way around.

Bottom line?

You don't need more time. You need to manage the time you already have like it matters. Because it does.

Success doesn't come from staying busy. It comes from making what matters, matter, every single day.

Chapter 8: Not Knowing Who Your Real Customer Is

Let us say this as clearly as we can...

If you don't know who your customer is, your business doesn't stand a chance.

We're not trying to be dramatic. We're just being honest.

Because this mistake, right here, is one of the *most common* and *most costly* traps that online business owners fall into. And the scary part is, that most people don't even realize they're doing it.

They create a course, launch a service, write blog posts, and record podcasts... but it's all aimed at this blurry, undefined crowd called "everyone."

They think being broad will help them reach more people. But in reality?

If you're trying to speak to everyone, you're connecting with no one.

"But My Product Could Help a Lot of People"

We hear this all the time.

And you know what? You might be right. Your product or service *could* help a lot of people.

But that's not the point.

You don't need a lot of people, you need the *right* people. The ones who are already searching for what you offer. The ones who are feeling the pain you solve. The ones who will *actually pay you* to make that pain go away.

You need to know who they are, what keeps them up at night, what language they use, and where they're already hanging out online.

Otherwise, you're guessing. And in business, guessing costs you time, energy, and money.

He Learned This the Hard Way

When Frank first started out online, he thought, "Hey, websites are for everybody." And technically, they are. Every business needs a website, right?

So he cast a wide net. He said yes to every type of client, mechanics, coaches, churches, authors, e-commerce stores. You name it, he built it.

And while that kept him busy, it didn't gain him *traction.*

Why? Because he was never positioned as an expert for *anyone.* He was just a generalist in a sea of generalists. Every new client was starting from scratch. No word-of-mouth momentum. No real connection.

It wasn't until he got specific, until he figured out who he loved working with, who he could help the most, and who *valued* the way he worked, that things really clicked.

- His messaging got clearer.
- His referrals got stronger.
- His income got better.
- And, let's be honest, his stress went way down.

People Pay for Relevance, Not General Advice

When your customer sees your message and thinks, "Wow… it's like they're reading my mind," that's when they start paying attention.

That's when you stand out from the noise.

But you can't get that kind of connection if you're not clear on who they are. Not just demographics, but *real-world details.*

- What are they struggling with right now?
- What would they type into Google at 2 AM when they can't sleep?
- What have they tried before that didn't work?
- What are they willing to invest in to solve it?

If you can't answer those questions, you're not ready to market. You're just shouting into the void.

The "Customer Avatar" Trap

Now, we know some of you have done those exercises where you create a "customer avatar" named Sally who drives a red SUV, shops at Target, and drinks oat milk lattes.

That's cute. But it's not enough.

Knowing what coffee she drinks won't help you sell more unless you understand *why* she buys what she buys and *what triggers her to act*.

You don't need a fictional backstory. You need real insight into the emotions, frustrations, and desires that drive your actual buyer.

That kind of clarity gives you power. It helps you write better copy, build better offers, and create marketing that actually sticks.

Your Action Step

Take 15 minutes today and dig into this:

- Who is the *best* person for what you offer? Not just *who could use it*, but who is actively searching, ready, and willing to pay for a solution?

- What do they believe about their problem?

- What's the cost of them *not* solving it?

- What have they already tried?

Talk to real people. Look at your past clients. Study the words your audience actually uses in forums, Facebook groups, and product reviews.

Because once you know who you're talking to, everything else gets easier.

Bottom line?

You can't serve the right customer if you don't know who they are. And you can't grow a business by guessing who might care.

So figure it out. Get specific. Then build everything, your message, your offers, your site, around that person.

Trust us. When you speak to *them*, they'll hear you loud and clear.

Chapter 9: Over-Researching and Under-Executing

We'll be the first to admit... We love learning.

New tools. New marketing strategies. The latest tactics from top entrepreneurs. You name it, We've probably taken the course, watched the webinar, read the book, or bookmarked the YouTube video.

But here's what we've learned after decades in the online business world:

> **More information isn't the problem.**
> **Lack of execution is.**

And if that hit a little close to home, good. Because this one matters.

Research Feels Productive, but It's Often Just Procrastination

Look, we get it. Doing research feels like you're "working on the business."

You're digging into the best email platforms...
Comparing checkout tools... Reading every blog post on building a lead magnet...
Thinking about doing a podcast, after you watch ten

more tutorials on how to name it, brand it, and set up the gear.

You're constantly *preparing* to take action.

But guess what? **You're still standing in place.**

At some point, more input becomes a crutch. A way to avoid the discomfort of actually *doing the thing.*

It's safe to watch, read, and plan.
It's risky to ship, publish, or launch.

And that's exactly why most people stay stuck in learning mode.

"But I Don't Want to Get It Wrong…"

Let us tell you something that most of the gurus won't:

You *will* get some of it wrong. That's part of the process. It's how you learn what works, for *your* audience, *your* offer, and *your* voice.

"I never lose.
I either win or learn."
- *Nelson Mandela*

We'd rather you launch something messy and start collecting real-world feedback than spend six months making it "perfect" in isolation… only to realize nobody wants it.

You don't learn by waiting. You learn by moving.
Refining.
Adjusting. Repeating.

You don't need another checklist right now. You need momentum.

We've Been Guilty of It Too

Do you think just because we've written books and built a few successful businesses we're immune to this? Nope.

There have been seasons where we've convinced ourselves we were just being "thorough." Researching tools. Comparing platforms. Mapping out a plan for our plans.

Do you know what snapped Bret out of it?

He looked at the whiteboard in his office, full of ideas he *hadn't* launched, and realized something hard: **information wasn't his problem. Execution was.**

The minute he stopped second-guessing and just *started*, progress happened fast. Was it perfect? Not even close.
But it was real. It was live. And it started producing results he could build on.

The truth is, that a lot of people hide behind research because it gives them an excuse not to fail.

"If I never launch, I can't flop."
"If I never hit publish, I can't be judged."
"If I stay in learning mode, I can't be exposed."

But here's the flip side of that...

If you never act, you'll never win.

All those big-name entrepreneurs you look up to? They're not where they are because they know everything. They're there because they acted, adjusted, and kept going.

You don't need to know everything to get started. You just need to start.

Your Action Step

Here's what we want you to do:

Look at the last business-related thing you consumed, a course, a video, an article. Ask yourself:

> Did I take action on it, or did I just file it
> away in my "someday" folder?

If it's sitting there collecting digital dust, pick *one* action you can take from it today. Just one. Doesn't have to be big. But do something that creates movement.

Also, take a break from consuming for a few days. No new content. No new tools. Just you and the task you've been putting off.

Start small. But start.

Bottom line?

You don't need more research. You need more doing.

You've got the knowledge. You've got the tools. Now you just need the guts to hit "go."

So stop stalling. Stop planning your next plan. Launch it. Test it. Learn from it. Then make it better.

That's how real businesses are built.

Chapter 10: Fear of Failing in Public, So You Never Launch

This one hits deep for a lot of folks. Not because they don't have the skills. Not because their idea isn't solid. Not because they can't figure out the tech.

It's fear. Plain and simple.

More specifically, it's the **fear of failing in front of other people.**

So they wait. And tweak. And revise. And wait some more.

Until eventually, the idea just fades. Not because it was a bad idea, but because it never even got the chance to *be tested.*

"What If No One Buys?"

"What If I Look Stupid?"

"What Will People Think?"

Do you ever hear those voices in your head?

You're about to post your offer, but your finger hovers over the mouse. You've got the email written, but you reread it for the 10th time.

You recorded a video, but you tell yourself it's not "good enough" yet.

Let us tell you something that might free you up a little:

Everyone feels this way at some point.

Even the "big names" you admire. Even the people making six or seven figures. Even us.

Putting yourself out there is scary. You're exposing your ideas, your work, your voice, and yes, there's always a chance people won't respond the way you hoped.

But here's the bigger truth:

> **Fear doesn't mean stop. Fear means
> step.**

You're Not Afraid of Failing, You're Afraid of Being *Seen* Failing

Let's be honest. If you launched a product and no one knew about it, you'd be bummed, but you'd survive. You'd try again.

What really holds people back is the *visibility* of failure.

"What if people see me try... and it doesn't work?"

That fear has killed more businesses than bad marketing ever has.

But let's flip it around for you:

What if people see you try… and they're inspired by your guts?

What if they don't laugh, but they cheer you on?

What if they become customers, not critics?

You can't find out unless you launch.

The First Version Will Never Be Perfect, And That's the Point

Newsflash: your first launch is going to be messy. You'll miss something. A button won't work. The copy might feel a little off. Welcome to the club. That's normal.

Nobody nails it out of the gate.

The people who win are the ones who launch anyway. They get feedback. They adjust. They get better. And because they're in motion, they build momentum.

Meanwhile, is the person still hiding behind perfection? They're still polishing an offer no one's ever seen.

We've Been There Too

Bret remembers the first time he launched a training of his own. He had worked behind the scenes on dozens of big launches, but when it was *his name* on the product?

Different story.

He felt exposed. Nervous. Unsure. He started second-guessing everything. Should he change the price? Should he re-record the videos? Is the sales page clear enough?

But he launched anyway. And you know what? It wasn't perfect. But it got results. And more importantly, it *started something.*

That launch led to the next one. That course led to more clients. And the momentum built from there.

If he had waited for perfection, he'd still be waiting.

Perfection Is the Enemy of Progress

Several years ago Bret was involved with the creation of course on seminar marketing. It was a team effort and a fantastic product was created.

But there was one team member who insisted every "I" be dotted and "T" crossed twenty times. It had to be "perfect." Well, month after month passed by and the launch kept getting pushed back.

The need for perfection totally killed the enthusiasm and momentum of the project team.

Even though the product did eventually get launched it never performed in the market as well as it should have because of that loss of momentum.

What's the Cost of Staying Silent?

Here's the real danger: the longer you wait to launch, the more weight that fear starts to carry.

And the more pressure you put on the launch to be *perfect*.

At some point, the fear of failing becomes more powerful than the desire to succeed. That's when people give up. They walk away from a business that could've worked, but they never gave it a real shot.

Don't let that be you.

Your Action Step

- What's the thing you've been sitting on?
- The offer you've mapped out but haven't shared?
- The post you've written but never published?

Launch it.

Today. Not tomorrow. Not "after you fix a few things." Hit publish. Send the email. Make the offer.

Yes, it's scary. But do it anyway, *especially* because it's scary.

That's where the growth happens.

Bottom line?

You don't get confidence first. You get confidence *by launching*. You don't get it right the first time. You *learn* by doing.

The world doesn't need your perfect product. It needs your *real* one.

So stop waiting for the fear to go away. Launch scared. Launch messy. Just **launch.**

Here's a little postscript for this chapter

Bret once had a client in the Forex niche who was launching a new product. Based on their previous launches the launch would generate anywhere from a few hundred thousand to over a million dollars.

Launch day came and they opened up their online cart and sales began to roll in. Things were looking good. Then, suddenly out of nowhere, their merchant account provider froze their merchant account.

Bret's client had forgotten to contact their provider to notify them they were doing a new product launch and would be generating greater than the usual number of sales.

You see, when you set up a merchant account you specify an average ticket price and an expected monthly volume. When you suddenly have a massive spike in sales that they aren't expecting it raises a major red flag for them. And they can freeze your account to protect themselves from possible fraud.

If the client had simply picked up the phone and contacted their provider to notify them what was going on the provider would have been fine with it. But they didn't call.

This mistake cost the client an estimated $300-$400 THOUSAND dollars worth of sales. Ouch.

Website & Tech Mistakes

Because if your digital foundation is broken, everything else falls apart.

Your website isn't just a brochure, it's your storefront, your sales rep, your customer service agent, and your brand ambassador all rolled into one.

And yet, way too many business owners treat it like an afterthought.

In this section, we'll dig into the most common mistakes that quietly kill trust, frustrate visitors, and cost you sales, from slow load times and sloppy mobile design to weak security and missing calls-to-action.

You don't have to be a tech expert to fix these. You just need to know what matters, and make it work for you, not against you.

These chapters will help you stop fighting with your website... and start using it to grow your business.

Chapter 11: Using a Slow, Poorly Built Website

Imagine this, you've poured your heart and soul into developing what you feel is a picture-perfect website. Not to mention your time and money. You've even done what most people skip: you created an actual traffic generation plan. And guess what? It's working. You're *getting* visitors.

But here's the problem...

- They're not buying
- They're not signing up
- They're not sticking around

You're watching the traffic come in, and bounce right back out. And yeah, it's frustrating. It's depressing. You start wondering, *What's wrong with my offer? My copy? My product?*

So you dig deeper. You check your site analytics and discover something alarming:

> **The average visitor is staying on your site for less than five seconds.**

Five seconds. That's barely enough time to read your headline, let alone understand the value of your product or service.

So what's happening? It could be a few things... but one of the biggest culprits, by far, is this: **Your website is slow.**

And these days? Slow equals *dead*.

People expect things to load instantly. If your site takes more than a couple of seconds to pop up, they're already gone, off to your competitor who *didn't* make them wait.

Worse yet? Google notices too. A slow site doesn't just hurt your user experience, it kills your search rankings.

If you want to check your own site's speed, tools like GTmetrix, Pingdom, or Google PageSpeed Insights can give you the brutal truth in just a few clicks.

Ideally, your site should load in **2 seconds or less**. Anything longer than that? You're losing visitors, leads, and sales, guaranteed.

So, What Slows a Site Down?

Let's look at the usual suspects:

1. Cheap or shared hosting
2. Large, uncompressed images
3. Too many plugins or scripts
4. Bloated WordPress themes
5. No caching or speed optimization
6. Unnecessary animations or design elements

Now let's break these down.

1. Cheap or Shared Hosting

That bargain $3/month hosting plan might seem like a great deal, until your site loads like it's running on dial-up.

With shared hosting, your site competes for resources with hundreds (sometimes thousands) of other sites on the same server. If one of them has a spike in traffic or bad code, *you* pay the price in load time.

Upgrading to quality, managed WordPress hosting can dramatically speed things up. It's not a cost, it's an investment in performance.

2. Large, Uncompressed Images

You wouldn't upload a billboard-sized graphic to display a thumbnail, but people do it all the time.

Huge image files are one of the biggest reasons websites lag. They eat up bandwidth and slow the initial page load.

Use image compression tools like TinyPNG, ImageOptim, or built-in WordPress plugins like ShortPixel or Smush to cut down on file sizes without sacrificing quality.

3. Too Many Plugins or Scripts

Every plugin you add to your site brings its own set of scripts, styles, and sometimes database calls. Multiply that by 20 or 30 plugins and suddenly your site's trying to load like it's wearing ankle weights.

Keep plugins lean. Use only what's essential. And delete the ones you're not actively using, they still slow things down even when deactivated.

4. Bloated WordPress Themes

Some themes are packed with bells, whistles, sliders, and options you'll never use, but they still load every time someone visits your site.

Choose a lightweight, speed-optimized theme instead. Astra, GeneratePress, or Kadence are great choices that won't bog down your pages.

5. No Caching or Speed Optimization

Without caching, every time someone visits your site, your server has to fetch and build the page from scratch. That takes time.

Caching stores a version of your site so it loads much faster for repeat visitors. Add a caching plugin like WP

Rocket or W3 Total Cache, and you'll see a noticeable speed bump.

Bonus tip: Use a CDN (Content Delivery Network) like Cloudflare to serve your content from servers *closer* to your visitors, reducing load time even more.

6. Unnecessary Animations or Fancy Design Effects

Sure, that background video and 3D carousel look cool… but if they're slowing your site down, they're costing you conversions.

Your visitors aren't there to be entertained by spinning icons. They're there to solve a problem.

If it doesn't support the message or the call-to-action, ditch it.

Don't Let Speed Kill Your Business

Every one of the issues we just covered is fixable. Most are avoidable from the start.

But ignoring them? That's like building a beautiful storefront, then locking the door and wondering why nobody's buying.

Your Action Step

Run a speed test on your homepage. Then on your sales page. Then on your blog.

Make a list of what's slowing things down, and fix it.

Start with hosting, then tackle images, plugins, and caching. You don't have to be a developer to make real improvements, you just have to *pay attention*.

Because performance isn't a luxury anymore. It's the price of admission.

Bottom line?

A slow website doesn't just frustrate your visitors, it *repels* them.

Speed up your site. Clean up the junk. Optimize every element. Because your business shouldn't be losing sales while your site tries to load.

Chapter 12: Relying Entirely on Social Media and Not Owning Your Platform

While posting content on social media can be a valuable part of the marketing mix for your business one must realize its limitations. It does offer you the opportunity to connect with your desired target audience and engage in direct discussion with them.

However, there are also disadvantages you must consider as you ascertain how to best take advantage of social media marketing. These include:

1. Social media can be extremely time-consuming

Cranking out regular content on multiple social media platforms takes time. Significant time. Are you creating videos? Writing blog posts? Creating checklists? Any of these take time. Time that could possibly be spent on other important aspects of your business.

2. You've got to be prepared for potential negative feedback

You better have a thick skin if you're going all in on social media. Some people will like you and others won't. And that's okay. But any negative feedback is out there for all the world to see and can tarnish your reputation.

4. The rules are constantly changing

What posts a social media platform displays to your followers is totally beyond your control. The algorithms that guide what is shown and not shown change on a regular basis.

5. It's hard to stand out

Your posts are just a single drop in an entire ocean of content that is posted every second on social media platforms. For example, the average half-life of an "X" post (formerly Twitter) is just 24 minutes. Good luck on your post being seen.

6. Hard to measure your return on investment

Everything you do for marketing has a cost associated with it – whether it's time or money. While you can easily track "likes" or the number of comments a post receives, can you easily track whether any of those led to an actual sale for your business?

7. You are not in control

You having control of your own email list of prospects is critical to the long-term success of your online business.

Your goal should be to drive people from your social media platforms to your own website where you can capture their email. Then you'll have the ability to directly reach out to these folks rather than just hope they see one of your social media posts. If you've been involved in marketing at all during your career you've probably heard the phrase "The Money's in the List." So true.

A properly conceived social media strategy can still be a valuable part of your marketing mix, but it's essential to recognize its limitations and manage them accordingly.

Your Action Step

1.) Evaluate all the major social media platforms and determine which ones the clients you want to attract hang out in.

2.) Develop a social media calendar for each of the platforms you're going to be active on. Decide what type of content you'll be releasing when in advance.

3.) If you don't have a way on your website to capture a prospect's email address then develop a lead magnet to begin building your own list.

4.) Construct an appropriate automated follow-up email sequence to go out to those people who opt into your email list.

Bottom line?

Social media is your billboard. Your website and email list? That's your storefront.

Own the storefront. Control the relationship. And stop giving your business to an algorithm that doesn't care if you succeed.

Chapter 13: Failing to Collect Email Addresses from Day One

If we could go back and change *one thing* in our early days of building online businesses, this would be it.

We would have started building our email lists from Day One. Not Day 100. Not "once everything was perfect." Not "after we finish the course."

Day. One.

Because here's the deal…

> **Your email list is one of the only assets you truly *own* online.**

You don't control Facebook. You don't own Instagram. TikTok can ban your account tomorrow. Google can change the algorithm next week.

But your email list? That's yours.

And if you're not collecting emails from the start, you're leaving opportunity, and money, on the table *every single day.*

"I Don't Want to Be Spammy…"

Let's just clear this up real quick.

Sending valuable, helpful, relevant content to people who *asked* to hear from you isn't spam. That's service. That's relationship-building. That's business.

You're not spamming. You're staying on top of mind.

People need multiple touchpoints before they buy. They don't always purchase on the first visit. Or the second. Or even the fifth.

But if you've got their email? You have a chance to follow up. Build trust. Share more value. Make another offer.

Without that list? You've got nothing but hope they remember your URL. (They won't.)

Email Still Converts Better Than Anything Else

We know it's not the shiny new platform. We know it's not as trendy as going viral on Reels.

But if you look at the actual numbers? **Email marketing still outperforms social media in almost every category.**

Higher click-through rates. More targeted messaging. Better open rates than your average organic post gets visibility.

And the kicker? The people on your list *want* to hear from you. They've already raised their hand. That's gold.

But you've got to give them a way to do that.

Start Small, But Start

Don't overthink it. You don't need a massive funnel or a 9-part autoresponder to get started.

You need two things:

1. **A reason for people to give you their email** - This could be a free guide, a checklist, a short training, an exclusive discount, whatever gives your ideal visitor a *quick win*.

2. **A place to capture it** - That means an opt-in form. On your homepage. In your blog posts. On landing pages. Even in your footer.

Make it easy. Make it obvious. And for the love of conversions, don't just say "Join My Newsletter."

Nobody wants more email. But they *do* want solutions. They want insight. They want value. Offer that.

We've Seen the Difference Firsthand

We've worked with clients who had *thousands* of daily visitors and no list. Tons of traffic, but no way to follow up, no ongoing communication, no community.

They thought they were doing fine… until traffic dropped.

Suddenly, there was no backup plan. No one to promote to. No way to recover quickly.

Then we added a simple opt-in strategy, and within weeks, they had a growing list, better engagement, and most importantly, **control** over their business again.

That's the power of a list.

Your Action Step

If you haven't started building your list yet, do it *today*.

- Pick a tool (Mailerlite, ConvertKit, Active Campaign, AWeber, Flodesk, whatever works for you)
- Create a simple lead magnet (think checklist, PDF, or video)
- Put an opt-in form on your homepage *above the fold*
- Mention it in your content, videos, and emails

- Set up a short welcome message to thank people and start the relationship

Then start growing that list, one subscriber at a time.

Because every name you collect? That's someone who trusted you enough to stay in touch.

That's not just a lead. That's *leverage.*

Bottom line?

If you're not collecting email addresses, you're building a business with no follow-up and no foundation.

Don't wait for "someday." Start now. Because your future income may depend on the list you start building today.

Chapter 14: Not Securing Your Site (No SSL, Outdated Plugins, Weak Passwords)

Let's be honest... Most people don't think about website security until something goes wrong.

They assume they're too small to be a target. They think their site's not "important enough" for hackers. Or they believe that if their site's up and running, everything must be fine.

Until it's not.

Then comes the email:

> "Hey... my site's down. It says it's been compromised. What do I do?"

Or worse,

They don't even *know* their site's been hacked until their customers start getting spammed, their search rankings tank, or their checkout pages redirect somewhere shady.

We've seen it all. And 90% of the time? **It could have been prevented.**

You Are a Target,
Even If You Think You're Not

Here's what most people don't understand:

Hackers don't sit around handpicking big-name websites to go after. They run automated bots that scan the internet 24/7 looking for easy targets.

Outdated plugins? Weak admin passwords? No SSL certificate? That's like leaving your doors unlocked and putting a sign out front that says, "Hey, come on in!"

It doesn't matter if you're a blogger, a coach, a local business, or just running a landing page, you're fair game. And if they can't get to you? They'll use your site to get to someone else.

SSL: Not Optional Anymore

If your site still shows "Not Secure" in the browser bar, that's a problem. Not just for security, but for trust.

Visitors see that warning and bounce. Google sees it and punishes your rankings. And if you're trying to take payments or collect emails without SSL? That's a deal-breaker.

Getting an SSL certificate is simple, most hosting companies offer it for free. You just have to *turn it on* and make sure your site redirects to the secure version.

If you haven't done that yet, stop reading and go fix it. I'll wait.

Outdated Plugins: The Digital Equivalent of Rusty Locks

WordPress is a great platform. We use it all the time. But it's only as secure as the tools you install on it.

And plugins? They're like little doors into your site.

When you don't update them, you're basically leaving those doors open, and sometimes wide open. Especially if the plugin is no longer supported or has known vulnerabilities.

Frank has cleaned up sites infected through abandoned plugins that hadn't been updated in years. The worst part? The site owners *thought* they were being careful. They just didn't think updates mattered.

They do. They always do.

Weak Passwords:
Still One of the Biggest Risks

It's 2025, and people are still using passwords like "admin123" or "password1."

Listen, we love simplicity too, but if your login is easy to guess, your site is easy to breach.

Use a strong, unique password. Use two-factor authentication if your tools allow it. And for the love of all things digital, **don't use "admin" as your username.**

Hackers know that's the default. And guess what they try first? Yup.

We've Seen the Cost of Getting It Wrong

Frank had a client years ago whose membership site got hacked. Malware was injected. Pages redirected to a phishing scam. Search rankings dropped like a rock. Stripe froze their payment processing until the site was clean.

They lost trust, sales, and hours of sleep.

And it all could've been avoided with three simple steps:

- A secure password
- Regular plugin updates
- A simple malware scanner

Security isn't sexy. But it's essential.

Your Action Step

Today, yes, *today*, go check the following:

- Is your site using SSL (https:// with the lock icon)?
- Are all your plugins, themes, and core software up to date?
- Are you using a strong password for your admin login?
- Do you have a backup system in place (see Chapter 19)?
- Are you running a basic security plugin like Wordfence, iThemes Security, or Sucuri?

None of these take hours. And all of them can save you a massive headache later.

"An ounce of prevention is worth a pound of cure."

– *Benjamin Franklin*

Bottom line?

If your site isn't secure, it's not just risky, it's irresponsible. You wouldn't leave your storefront unlocked. Don't leave your digital doors wide open either.

Lock it down. Stay updated. And make sure your business is protected before something breaks.

Chapter 15: No Clear Call-to-Action Above the Fold

Let's get straight to the point, because your visitors sure are.

When someone lands on your website, you've got **about 5 seconds**, maybe less, to grab their attention and guide them to what's next.

And yet, one of the biggest mistakes we see on websites is this:

There's no clear call-to-action above the fold.

You know what we mean, right? "Above the fold" is just a fancy way of saying the part of your site that shows up *before* someone scrolls. It's prime real estate. The first impression. Your digital handshake.

And it's often completely wasted.

The "Look Around and Figure It Out" Approach Doesn't Work

Too many homepages are cluttered with vague headlines, stock photos, or branding fluff, and no clear direction on what to do next.

It's like walking into a store and not knowing where the checkout, help desk, or even the *products* are. Nobody's there to greet you. No signs. Just… figure it out.

How long are you sticking around? Not long.

Now imagine your visitor. They're scanning fast. They're juggling tabs. They're distracted. If they don't immediately see *what this site is about* and *what they're supposed to do*, they're gone.

- No opt-in
- No sale
- No click
- No chance

One Page. One Purpose.

Here's something we teach over and over again:

Every page on your site should have one primary job.

Not three. Not five. **One.**

That job might be to:

- Get someone to join your list
- Book a free consultation
- Buy a product
- Download a lead magnet

- Watch a video
- Register for a webinar

Whatever it is, that action needs to be obvious, and it needs to be front and center.

Not buried halfway down the page. Not hidden behind clever language. Not only on the contact page.

Right up top. Visible. Clear. Tap-able. Clickable. Actionable.

Clarity Beats Clever

We get it, everyone wants to sound unique. You want your brand to stand out. But sometimes, in trying to sound cool, people get *too* clever with their messaging.

Instead of saying "Start Your Free Trial" or "Book Your Session," they go with things like:

- "Let's Get You Started!"
- "Discover the Possibilities"
- "Your Journey Begins Here"

And while those sound nice, they don't answer the question:

What am I supposed to do right now?

Don't make people guess. Don't make them scroll. Don't make them think harder than they need to.

Frank's Watched This in Real Time

He's done screen recordings and heatmaps for client sites, and it's amazing (and painful) to watch.

Visitors land on the homepage, look around… and click nothing.

Not because they aren't interested. But because there's no obvious next step. They're being asked to *figure it out*, and most don't bother.

Now compare that to a site with a bold, above-the-fold call-to-action, something like:

- "Get My Free Guide Now"
- "Schedule Your Free Call"
- "Claim Your 20% Discount"

Click-throughs jump. Leads go up. Conversions improve.

Why? Because it's clear. And clarity builds trust.

Your Action Step

Look at your homepage right now.

Can a first-time visitor immediately tell:

1. What you do
2. Who it's for
3. What to do next

And is that next step *above the fold*, on both desktop and mobile?

If it's not, fix that first. It's one of the easiest wins you'll ever get in your online business.

Don't bury your best offer. Don't hide your call-to-action.
Put it where it matters, right where people are looking.

Bottom line?

If you don't tell your visitors what to do, they'll do nothing.

Make it obvious. Make it easy. Make it unmissable, *above the fold.*

Because clicks don't happen by accident. They happen when you guide the way.

Chapter 16: Building on Free Platforms That Limit Scalability

Let's talk about "free."

Because free sounds great when you're just starting out, right?

- Free website builder
- Free eCommerce store
- Free course platform
- Free email marketing tool

You sign up, start plugging in your content, drag a few blocks around, and boom, you've got a business. Or so it seems.

But here's the problem...

> **That free platform you're building your business on?**
>
> **It wasn't built for *your* growth, it was built for *theirs*.**

And if you're not careful, you'll hit a wall faster than you can say "upgrade required."

Free Always Comes with a Cost

Now don't get me wrong, we get why people start with free tools. Money's tight. You're just testing things out. You want to move fast.

And in the beginning? That can be okay, as long as you understand what you're trading. Because while you're saving a little money upfront, you're often paying for it in:

- **Limited features** (Want to customize your checkout? Nope.)
- **Forced branding** ("This site was made with FreeSiteBuilder123!")
- **Lack of ownership** (Can't export your content. Can't control your data.)
- **Platform rules** (They can suspend you anytime, for any reason.)
- **SEO limitations** (Free platforms rarely give you full control over meta tags, URLs, or load speed.)
- **No real support** (Unless you upgrade... or beg in the forums.)

So you get your business rolling, you build some momentum, and suddenly you're boxed in.

Want to switch? Good luck migrating your content. Want to grow? Time to rebuild, *from scratch*, on a platform that actually lets you scale.

Businesses Have Been Trapped

We don't how many times someone has said:

> "I started on [insert free platform] and now I can't do XYZ... Can you help me move everything over?"

And what should've been a simple upgrade turns into a full-blown rebuild. Lost content, broken links, layout issues, customer confusion, you name it.

All because they started building a business on top of a foundation they didn't own.

Look, we understand the appeal of "quick and easy," but ask yourself:

> **Would you build a house on land someone else controls, and could take away any time?**

Because that's what a free platform is. You don't own it. You're just renting space, and your landlord can change the rules whenever they want.

Build Like You Mean to Grow

If you're serious about your business, then you've got to treat it like a business. That means choosing tools and platforms that give you:

- Ownership
- Control
- Flexibility
- Portability
- Scalability

Even if it costs you a little upfront, it saves you *a lot* down the road.

Platforms like WordPress (self-hosted), Shopify (if you're in eCommerce), or even building a simple email list on a trusted provider, that's how you build with growth in mind.

You want something that grows *with* you, not something you outgrow in six months.

Your Action Step

If you're currently using a free platform, take a hard look at what you *can't* do.

What happens when you want to:

- Add a new offer?
- Create a custom checkout?
- Integrate with your CRM or payment gateway?
- Remove their branding?
- Export your customer list?

If any of that sounds complicated, or flat-out impossible, it's time to start planning your move to a more scalable solution.

The longer you wait, the harder that transition gets.

Bottom line?

Free is fine when you're learning. But if you're building a real business, you need real tools.

Don't build your future on someone else's platform. Own your brand. Own your site. Own your growth.

Because *free* will cost you more than you think.

Chapter 17: Not Testing How Your Site Looks on Mobile

Let us hit you with a stat right out of the gate:

> **More than half of your website visitors are coming from a mobile device.**

And in some industries? That number is even higher.

So if you're only building and reviewing your website on a desktop screen… You're designing for the minority.

That's like building a retail store optimized for people over 7 feet tall. Sure, it *works* for them. But everyone else? They're squinting, scrolling, and getting frustrated before they even see your offer.

Bottom line?

> **If your website doesn't work on mobile, it doesn't work.**

"But It Looked Great on My Laptop…"

Yeah… that's the trap.

You spend hours designing your site on your nice big monitor. Everything lines up. The fonts are readable. The buttons look slick. The layout feels dialed in.

Then you open it on your phone and...

- The headline is so small you need reading glasses
- The text stretches on forever
- The call-to-action button is halfway off the screen
- Images don't scale
- Menus don't open
- Somehow your logo is the size of a postage stamp

At that point, your visitor has one thought: *"I'll come back later."*

(And let's be honest... they won't.)

Google Cares About Mobile, So Should You

Here's something a lot of business owners don't realize: Google ranks your website *based on its mobile version first.*

Not desktop. **Mobile.**

If your mobile experience is slow, clunky, or confusing, it's not just hurting your conversions, it's hurting your visibility too.

And don't even get me started on page speed. Those heavy images and bloated scripts that look "cool" on a desktop computer? They're *destroying* your mobile load time.

People won't wait. If your site doesn't load in a couple of seconds, they're gone.

We've Seen Beautiful Sites Fail on Phones

Frank once had a client bring him a site they had paid thousands for. It looked gorgeous on the desktop, with high-end design, animated sections, full-width imagery, and all the bells and whistles.

But on mobile? It was a mess.

Text over images, buttons you couldn't tap, videos that wouldn't play, and entire sections that just didn't show up.

The kicker? Most of their traffic was coming from mobile ads. So basically, they were paying to send people to a site that didn't work on the device those people were using.

He fixed the mobile experience, and guess what? Their conversion rate tripled.

No new offer. No new copy. Just a site that *worked* for the people using it.

Don't Assume, Test

This one's simple. You can't assume your site looks good on mobile just because it *should*. You've got to test it.

And not just once when you launch. Every time you update a page, change a theme, or install a new plugin, check it on your phone.

Better yet, check it on *multiple* phones. Android and iPhone. Big screens and small screens. Because different devices can behave differently.

And while you're at it, go through your entire funnel. Opt-in. Checkout. Booking page. All of it. You might be shocked at how many steps are broken, confusing, or just plain missing on mobile.

Your Action Step

Take your phone out right now. Open your homepage. Scroll through slowly.

Ask yourself:

- Can I tell what this site is about in the first few seconds?
- Is the text easy to read without zooming in?
- Are the images scaled properly?
- Is the menu easy to use?

- Can I clearly see, and tap, the main call-to-action?

If the answer to any of those is "no," make it a priority to fix it. Because if your site isn't mobile-friendly, it's not customer-friendly.

Bottom line?

Don't build for your desk, build for your *user*.

Because in today's world, your mobile site *is* your website.

So check it. Fix it. And make sure it's working for the people who matter most, your visitors.

Chapter 18: Overdesigning Instead of Focusing on Clarity

Let's say something that might ruffle a few designer feathers…

Pretty doesn't pay the bills.

Don't get us wrong, We love clean, professional design. A good-looking site can build trust, show off your brand, and make a great first impression.

But here's the hard truth most online business owners need to hear:

Design should never get in the way of clarity.

And yet, time after time, we see business owners obsess over color palettes, fonts, gradients, scroll effects, background videos, parallax sliders, and other "shiny" stuff… while completely ignoring the most important thing:

Can the visitor figure out what you do, who it's for, and what to do next, within five seconds?

Because if the answer is no, it doesn't matter how slick your site looks. You're losing people before they even have a chance to become customers.

When Design Tries Too Hard

Here's what usually happens.

Someone builds a site, or hires someone to build it, and they want it to "pop." They want it to stand out. They want it to feel *next-level.*

So the homepage ends up packed with motion, animations, three different fonts, glowing buttons, spinning icons, and five sections that compete for attention.

And you know what your visitor sees?

Noise.

Too much going on. Too many choices. No clear direction.

And when people are overwhelmed online, they don't dig deeper... They *leave.* Fast.

Function First, Style Second

The purpose of your website isn't to impress, it's to **convert**.

It's there to deliver a message, build trust, and get the right person to take the next step. Whether that's opting in, booking a call, or buying something, it's all about movement.

Good design supports that. Bad design distracts from it.

You can have a beautiful site that performs horribly. Or a clean, simple one that out-converts the flashy sites all day long.

We've seen plain white pages with black text and a single buy button outperform $10,000 design jobs, *because the message was clear, the offer was solid, and the action was obvious.*

Frank Has Been Asked to "Make It Look More Impressive"

Let us tell you, Frank has had clients come to him with fully functioning websites and say, "Can you just make it look more… impressive?"

And his response is always the same:

> "Do you want it to *impress* people…
> or *convert* them?"

Because sure, he can add sparkle. He can add animation. He can make the logo spin while the button fades in from the top left corner of the screen…

But that doesn't mean it's going to get more signups.

Most of the time, he ends up *removing* stuff instead. Simplifying. Clarifying. Making the site easier to scan, easier to navigate, and way easier to act on.

And guess what? That's when the numbers go up.

You're Not Building for Designers, You're Building for Visitors

Nobody's coming to your site to admire your layout. They're coming to solve a problem. If your design doesn't make that solution obvious... you've missed the mark.

So ask yourself:

- Is my main message above the fold?
- Is my navigation simple and intuitive?
- Are my calls-to-action clear and consistent?
- Is there enough white space for things to breathe?
- Can someone understand what I do *without scrolling*?

If you're more concerned about your font pairing than your offer clarity, it's time to shift focus.

Your Action Step

Open your homepage right now and pretend you've never seen it before. Give yourself five seconds.

What jumps out? What's the headline? What's the next step you're supposed to take?

If you can't answer those questions quickly, imagine how confused your visitors must be.

Simplify it. Tighten your message. Strip away anything that doesn't help the visitor make a decision. You don't need to wow them with effects. You need to guide them to action.

Bottom line?

Don't let fancy get in the way of functional. Don't let "cool" override "clear."

Design with purpose. Build with clarity. And your site won't just look good, it'll actually *work*.

Chapter 19: Not Having a Backup and Disaster Recovery System

Let's talk about something nobody wants to think about... until it's too late.

- Your website goes down.
- Your server crashes.
- Your database gets corrupted.
- Your WordPress install gets hacked.
- Your hosting company has an outage.
- You click the wrong button and accidentally delete *everything*.

And just like that, *boom*, your entire online business grinds to a halt. No website. No sales. No leads. No traffic.

Now here's the real question:

If that happened today, could you recover?

If your answer is, "I think my hosting company takes care of that..." Or worse, "Uh... I don't know?"

You've got a problem.

You Don't Need a Backup... Until You Do

Look, we're not trying to scare you here. We're trying to *wake you up.*

Because we've seen it too many times. Smart people. Good businesses. Totally wiped out because they didn't have a solid backup and recovery plan in place.

They assumed their hosting company was handling it. They assumed their website was "too small" to be targeted. They assumed that because everything was working yesterday, it'd still be working tomorrow.

And then they lost it all.

- We've seen product creators lose entire courses
- We've seen bloggers lose years of content
- We've seen online stores disappear overnight, with no way to get the site back.

And the worst part? **It's 100% preventable.**

Backups Aren't Optional, They're Your Safety Net

Let's be clear: if your business *relies* on your website, then you need to take backups as seriously as you take making sales.

Because here's the truth:

**It's not a matter of *if* something will go wrong,
it's a matter of *when*.**

That's not being negative. That's just business. Plugins
conflict. Updates break things. Hackers get creative. And
even if you're not a tech person, you *still* need a plan.

Because of your business? Your content? Your customer
data?

That's your *digital storefront*. If you lose it, you lose
time, money, and most importantly, *trust*.

Hosting Isn't a Backup Plan

Now we know what some folks are thinking: "My
hosting company says they back everything up."

Maybe they do. But here's what they *don't* tell you:

- How often do those backups happen?
- How long are they stored?
- Whether you can access them when you need
  them
- If they'll even help you restore it without a
  support ticket backlog.

Let us tell you something we've learned the hard way:

If you're not in control of your own backup, you don't have one

You need your own system. Something you can access quickly. Something that doesn't rely on someone else's schedule or support response time.

And ideally, something that stores copies in *multiple* places, just in case one of those goes down too.

Years ago, one of Frank's sites got hit with a bad plugin conflict. Crashed the whole site. Completely wiped the database.

Luckily, he had just installed an automated backup system the month before. He restored it in minutes.

If he hadn't? That would've been weeks of rebuilding from scratch.

And trust us, rebuilding when you're stressed, behind, and losing income? That's not a fun place to be.

Your Action Step

If you don't already have one, get a reliable backup system in place today.

We're not saying you have to get fancy. There are plenty of solid tools out there like **UpdraftPlus**, **BlogVault**,

BackupBuddy, or even using automated services through platforms like **ManageWP**.

Set it to run automatically. Store backups in the cloud (Dropbox, Google Drive, Amazon S3, whatever works). And every so often, check that it's actually working. Don't assume it is. Open a file. Do a test restore on a staging site.

It's boring. It's technical. And it could save your entire business.

"Only the Paranoid Survive."

– Andy Grove, former CEO of Intel

Bottom line?

If you don't have a disaster recovery plan, you're gambling.
And eventually, the house always wins.

So stop hoping nothing goes wrong. Start preparing for when it does. Back it up. Lock it down. And sleep better knowing that if the worst happens… you've got a way back.

Chapter 20: Forgetting to Track Visitor Data and Behavior

We'll make this simple:

If you're not tracking what people are doing on your site, you're basically flying blind.

And we don't mean kind of blind like "I think that landing page is doing okay." We mean full-on, "lights off, windows closed, driving at night without headlights" blind.

Yet this is a mistake *so many* online business owners make.

They launch the site. They set up the offer. They even spend money sending traffic to it...

But they have no clue what's actually happening once people land on the page.

- How long do they stay?
- What links are they clicking?
- Where are they dropping off?
- Are they even scrolling?

No idea. Because they're not tracking any of it.

What You Don't Know *Is* Hurting You

Let us tell you, your website visitors are talking to you.

Not with words, but with clicks, scrolls, hesitations, and exits. They're telling you where they're confused. They're telling you what's working, and what isn't. They're literally showing you the roadblocks keeping them from buying.

But if you're not tracking behavior, you're not listening.

You're just guessing. And guessing is expensive.

Data Doesn't Lie, But Assumptions Do

You might *think* your call-to-action is clear. You might *believe* your pricing is obvious. You might *feel* like people are reading your sales page all the way through.

But without data, that's all it is, your best guess.

When you start using tools like Google Analytics, heatmaps, session recordings, or even simple conversion tracking, it's like turning the lights on.

You can *see* where people are dropping off. You can *see* which buttons get clicked. You can *see* which page gets all the traffic, and which one sends people running.

Suddenly, the "why isn't this working?" mystery gets a lot easier to solve.

Bret Has Made This Mistake Too

In his early days, he was so focused on getting a page launched, he'd forget to set up even the basics. No analytics. No tracking pixel. Nothing.

He'd run a promotion, send out emails, and just hope people were clicking through and buying. Sometimes they were. Sometimes they weren't. But he had no idea *why* either way.

It wasn't until he started using tracking tools that he realized one of his landing pages had a headline that was actually confusing people. The bounce rate was sky-high. People weren't even scrolling past the first section.

He made one small change to the headline, and conversions jumped. That's the power of tracking. One change based on real data can unlock the results you've been waiting for.

"But I Don't Want to Get Bogged Down in Numbers..."

Trust me, we hear that.

And yes, analytics dashboards can be overwhelming at first. But here's the thing, you don't need to be a data nerd. You just need to know enough to ask the right questions.

Start simple:

- Where are people coming from?
- How long are they staying?
- What page do they exit on?
- What content do they engage with most?

Even just knowing those four things can transform how you approach your site, your content, and your offers.

The goal isn't to drown in data. It's to **make better decisions** based on what people are actually doing, not what you hope they're doing.

Your Action Step

- If you haven't already, install Google Analytics
- Set up basic conversion tracking
- If you really want to see what's happening, use a heatmap tool like Hotjar or Microsoft Clarity

And then, check in weekly.

You don't have to be obsessed, but you *do* need to pay attention. Because data is one of the few business tools that gets smarter the more you use it.

Let it guide you. Let it surprise you. Let it tell you where your money is being left on the table.

Bottom line?

If you're not tracking behavior, you're not running a business, you're just making digital noise and hoping for the best.

Turn on the lights. Check the numbers. See what's working, and double down on it.

That's how you stop guessing and start growing.

Marketing Mistakes

Because even the best product won't sell itself.

You've got a solid offer. Maybe even a great one. But what if your marketing isn't clear, consistent, and targeted? It's like shouting into the wind.

This section covers the most common ways entrepreneurs fumble their marketing, by speaking to everyone (and connecting with no one), chasing followers instead of building relationships, or relying too heavily on platforms they don't control.

We're not here to make you a marketing guru overnight. We're here to help you avoid the costly mistakes that slow growth, confuse your audience, and drain your momentum.

Get ready to simplify your message, sharpen your strategy, and finally market with confidence.

Chapter 21: Trying to Market to Everyone (and Appealing to No One)

This one's tough love, but it needs to be said:

If your marketing is trying to reach everyone, it's connecting with no one.

We know, we know, when you're starting out, it feels like casting a wide net makes sense. "The more people I reach, the more sales I'll make," right?

But that's not how it works.

In fact, one of the biggest mistakes we see (and yes, we've made it ourselves) is trying to be everything to everyone... and ending up being *forgettable* to all of them.

Being Broad Feels Safe, but It's Dangerous

We get it. Narrowing your audience feels risky. You don't want to exclude anyone. You don't want to miss out on a sale. You think, "Well, this product could help *anyone*, so I'll just talk to *everyone*."

But here's the problem: when your message is generic, it doesn't resonate. It doesn't spark curiosity. It doesn't make someone stop scrolling, stop thinking about dinner, or stop checking their email and say, "Wait… they're talking to *me*."

Specificity is what gets attention. Clarity is what builds trust. Relevance is what drives action. And you can't have any of that if you're talking to the crowd.

"But What If I Niche Down Too Far?"

Let's flip that for you: **what if you finally reach the right people who are ready to buy because you finally spoke their language?**

Here's the truth: niching down doesn't shrink your opportunity, it *sharpens* it.

When you narrow your focus, you get crystal clear on:

- The problems you solve
- The people you serve
- The language they use
- The places they hang out
- The exact message that gets them to pay attention

That's not limiting. That's *laser targeting*, and it's how successful online businesses grow fast and consistently.

We've Seen This Over and Over Again

Frank once worked with a client who offered digital marketing services for "any business that needs more traffic."

That sounds great, right? Lots of businesses want more traffic.

But her website was a mess of vague promises: "Grow your brand. Get more visibility. Unlock your potential." Blah, blah, blah.

No one knew what she *actually* did, or if it was for them.

He helped her niche down. Focused on helping real estate professionals get seller leads through YouTube ads. Suddenly, the copy snapped into place. The offer was clear. The targeting was specific. And the results? Night and day.

She didn't just *sound* better, she finally connected with the right people.

Think of Your Audience Like a Conversation

When you're at a party and someone shouts, "Hey, everyone!", most people tune it out. But if they say, "Hey, Sarah, I've got something that could help with your bookkeeping problem..." Sarah's listening.

Your marketing needs to be that specific. It needs to feel personal, like a conversation, not a billboard.

And here's the cool part: when you market to a focused audience, people *outside* that group still see the value. They just see it more clearly because you've made it tangible.

Your Action Step

If you've been marketing too broadly, ask yourself this:

- Who *specifically* is my product or service best for?
- What problem are they trying to solve right now?
- What words do they use to describe that struggle?
- What result do they want most, and how can I position my offer around that?

Once you answer those questions, update your homepage, your opt-in offer, your emails, and *everything*, to speak directly to that person.

Stop shouting into the crowd. Start having a conversation with the person who's actually ready to work with you.

Bottom line?

Trying to appeal to everyone waters down your message. But when you speak directly to the right person, everything gets easier.

Your copy gets clearer. Your conversions go up. Your confidence grows. So define your audience, and start showing up like the expert they've been waiting for.

Chapter 22: Inconsistent Branding and Messaging

Ever walk into a store that looks one way on the outside… and completely different on the inside?

Like, the sign says "modern and upscale," but when you step in, it feels like a yard sale from 2003.

That jarring disconnect? That *"Wait, what am I looking at?"* moment? That's what happens when your **branding and messaging are inconsistent.**

And it's one of the easiest ways to lose trust online.

"Your brand is what other people say about you when you're not in the room."

– *Jeff Bezos*

Consistency Builds Confidence

Your brand is more than your logo. It's your tone, your visuals, your message, your values. It's how you handle your customer service. It's the *promise* you make to your audience, everywhere you show up.

And when that promise shifts from page to page or post to post, people get confused.

Your homepage says you serve entrepreneurs...
Your blog says you're for small business owners...
Your social media suddenly sounds like it's for influencers...
And your lead magnet? It's targeting stay-at-home parents.

Even if you've got great content, people don't know if it's *for them.* Confusion kills conversion.

Mixed Messages = Missed Opportunities

Let's put it plainly:

If your visuals, voice, and messaging don't line up, **you look like a mess.** And people don't buy from messy brands. They buy from businesses that seem professional, credible, and clear.

We've seen coaches with three different taglines floating around. We've seen brands using one color scheme on their site and a totally different one on social. And we've seen lead magnets that don't match the tone of the main offer at all.

It's like listening to a radio station that keeps changing genres mid-song. Nobody sticks around long.

"But I'm Just Figuring Things Out…"

Totally fair. Everyone evolves. Your brand will too.

But even while you're figuring it out, aim for cohesion. You don't have to have everything perfect, just **aligned.**

That means:

- Your message is the same on your homepage, sales pages, emails, and social.
- Your tone of voice feels like *you*, not a marketing robot on one page and a comedian on the next.
- Your visuals follow a clear pattern: same colors, same fonts, same feel.
- Your audience knows what you're about and who you're for, *instantly.*

You want people to say, "Oh yeah, that's totally their stuff." That's how trust is built.

Frank's Cleaned Up This Mess Before

Frank had a client come to him with great content, but scattered branding. Her site felt polished. Her emails felt casual. Her lead magnet was written in third person. Her social posts? All over the map.

He helped her pick a core message, cleaned up her visual style, and rewrote her bio and call-to-actions so everything *sounded like her.*

- Her engagement went up
- Her conversion rates jumped
- People started saying, "I feel like I know you."

That's the power of brand consistency.

Your Action Step

Do a quick audit.

- Does your website copy match the tone of your emails?
- Are your colors and fonts consistent across platforms?
- Is your core message, the "who you help and how", clear and repeated often?
- Can someone scroll your feed, open your site, or read your bio and *get you* in under 10 seconds?

If not, it's time to tighten things up.

Start with your core message. Make sure everything connects to that. Then clean up your visuals and voice so they all match the *feel* of your brand.

Bottom line?

Inconsistent branding doesn't just look unprofessional, it *feels* uncertain. And uncertainty repels buyers.

Be clear. Be cohesive. Make every part of your business look like it belongs to the same confident brand.

Chapter 23: Not Building a Lead Magnet or Funnel

Here's a simple question:

What happens when someone visits your website?

If your answer is "Well, hopefully, they look around and decide to buy something...", we need to talk.

Because *hope* is not a strategy. If your entire business relies on someone stumbling across your site, falling in love with your offer, and making a purchase on the spot then you're setting yourself up for disappointment.

People Rarely Buy on the First Visit

Even the most interested visitor needs time. Time to trust you. Time to think it over. Time to compare.

So, if you're not capturing their info the moment they arrive, *you're losing them.*

They'll click away. They'll forget your site. And your chance at building a relationship? Gone.

That's why you need a lead magnet. A lead magnet that feeds into a funnel.

What's a Lead Magnet, Anyway?

The simple answer is that: it's a reason for someone to give you their email address.

It could be:

- A checklist
- A cheat sheet
- A short guide
- A free video
- A mini-course
- A discount code
- A quiz
- Even just exclusive content

The key is this: it solves *one small, specific problem* your ideal customer has right now. Not later. Not "someday." Right. Now.

And Then... the Funnel Kicks In

Once they opt in, that's your opportunity to keep the conversation going.

This is where most folks drop the ball. They get the email, and then... silence. Or worse, they immediately send a pitch with no context, no value, no trust.

A funnel isn't just a sales tool; it's a relationship builder.

Start with a welcome email. Tell them who you are, what to expect, and how you can help. Follow up with value-packed content. Show your expertise. Then, *and only then*, make an offer.

You don't need a 47-email sequence. You need a short, strategic series that moves someone from curious… to confident… to customer.

"But Guys, I Don't Know What to Offer…"

Start with this:

- What's the #1 question people ask you?
- What's something you wish every prospect knew *before* a sales call?
- What's a common mistake your audience makes?

Answer that in a 1- or 2-page resource, and boom, you've got your first lead magnet. Don't overcomplicate it. You're not writing a novel. You're giving people a shortcut to a win.

We've Seen Businesses Turn Around Overnight

Frank helped one client create a simple one-page PDF: "7 Questions to Ask Before Hiring a Web Designer."

She promoted it on her homepage and in her social media bio. Within weeks, she had a growing email list, better leads, and people showing up to sales calls already trusting her.

Why? Because the lead magnet did the work of *pre-framing* the sale. That's the power of a funnel.

Your Action Step

If you don't have a lead magnet yet, pick one idea today and build it.

Then:

1. Add an opt-in form to your homepage
2. Set up a simple email sequence (3–5 emails is a great start)
3. Promote the lead magnet in your content, social, and email signature
4. Test it, track what's working, and refine it over time

You don't need perfection. You need *progress*.

Bottom line?

If you're not building a list and guiding people through a funnel, you're leaving leads (and money) on the table.
Stop waiting for visitors to magically convert.
Give them a reason to stay, and a clear path to follow.

That's how you turn traffic into trust... and trust into sales.

Chapter 24: Focusing Too Much on Social Media "Likes" Over Leads

You post something. It gets a few hearts, a couple of comments, and maybe even a share. Feels good, right?

But here's the question that really matters:

> **Did any of those "likes" turn into leads...**
> **or just give you a Dopamine hit?**

Listen, we're not here to knock social media. We use it too. It's great for visibility, engagement, and showing up where your audience hangs out.

But far too many business owners confuse *activity* with *progress*. They're chasing likes instead of leads. And it's killing their growth.

Vanity Metrics ≠ Business Growth

"Likes," "follows," and "shares" are nice to look at. They make you feel like you're doing something right. But you can't take likes to the bank.

You can't pay your mortgage with views. You can't scale your business on "Nice post!" comments.

Yet we see entrepreneurs pour hours, *days*, into posting, dancing for the algorithm, and tweaking captions... while completely ignoring their lead funnel, email list, or sales strategy.

If that's you, here's a truth bomb:

> **You don't need to be popular. You need to be profitable.**

Likes Don't Build Relationships, Conversations Do

A "like" is the lowest form of engagement. It's passive. It's lazy. It doesn't mean the person even read your post.

But a lead?

That's someone who trusted you enough to give their email. That's a potential customer. That's someone saying, "I'm interested. Tell me more."

If your content isn't designed to drive that kind of action, opt-ins, replies, clicks, downloads, then you're not using your platform strategically.

You're just performing.

Social Media Should *Feed* Your Funnel

Here's the shift: don't treat social media as the business. Treat it as the **bridge** to your business.

Every few posts, ask yourself:

- Is there a clear call-to-action?
- Am I driving traffic to my lead magnet or opt-in?
- Am I collecting contact info or just collecting likes?

Likes are rented attention. Your list is owned connection.

One you *hope* will work. The other, you *control*.

People Can Burn Out Chasing Engagement

Frank once had a client who posted multiple times a day across three platforms. Beautiful designs. Thoughtful captions. Consistent schedule.

She had 20,000+ followers and tons of "engagement."

But her list? A couple of hundred people. Her sales? Sporadic at best.

He helped her rework her content strategy to promote her lead magnet every week. They simplified her funnel and added CTAs to her posts and bio. In 90 days, her list grew by 2,500 leads, and sales followed right behind.

All because she stopped chasing applause and started building assets.

Your Action Step

Take a look at your last 10 posts. How many of them included a clear next step?

- "Download this free guide"
- "Join my email list here"
- "DM me for access to XYZ"
- "Click the link in the bio to get started"

If that number is close to zero, it's time to shift your strategy. Start creating content that drives traffic to your list, your offer, or your funnel, not just content that makes people smile and scroll.

Because while engagement is fun, *leads* are what grow your business.

Bottom line?

Likes won't pay the bills. Leads will.

So stop chasing the algorithm and start building something you own. Because popularity might feel good, but profitability *feels a whole lot better.*

Chapter 25: Over-Relying on One Traffic Source (e.g., Just Facebook Ads or Just SEO)

Here's a little story we've heard way too many times…

> "Everything was going great. Leads were coming in. Sales were up. Then overnight, BOOM, nothing."

What happened?

Facebook changed the rules. Google updated the algorithm. Their ad account got flagged. Their traffic dropped off a cliff.

All because they were depending on *one* source to feed their entire business.

That's not a strategy, that's a gamble.

And eventually, the house always wins.

Don't Build Your Business on One Lane

Imagine owning a restaurant that only gets foot traffic from one street. What happens when that street closes for construction? Or gets rerouted?

Now imagine that happening to your online business, but instead of construction, it's a platform shift, a pricing change, or an algorithm update.

That's what happens when you go all-in on just one traffic source.

Now don't get us wrong, **specializing can be smart**. You *should* master what works. But you also need to diversify.

Because the internet doesn't stand still. And what worked yesterday might not work tomorrow.

Businesses Have Been Wiped Out Overnight

We know a person who was killing it with Facebook ads. We're talking 6-figure months. But one day, Facebook flagged her account, for no clear reason, and everything stopped.

No ads. No traffic. No sales. And no backup plan.

We scrambled to build an email list from scratch, revive her SEO, and set up organic funnels, *after* the panic hit. It was fixable, but it was stressful. And it could've been avoided with a little diversification.

Your Traffic Portfolio Needs Balance

Think of your traffic sources like income streams. You wouldn't want all your revenue from a single client. Why? Because if they leave, you're in trouble.

Same with traffic. A smart business blends multiple channels:

- **Paid traffic** (Facebook, Google, YouTube ads)
- **Organic search** (SEO, blog content, YouTube videos)
- **Social media** (short-form, long-form, platforms you *own*)
- **Email marketing** (your *most* controllable asset)
- **Referral/affiliate traffic** (partnerships and recommendations)
- **Direct outreach** (podcasts, interviews, guest posts)

Each one supports the other. And if one slows down? You're still in the game.

Bret was co-founder of a company that built its entire 7-figure business off of attending live events and networking. No other proactive marketing was being done.

Then, COVID-19 hit and live events went away. The business' sales dropped dramatically because it didn't have any additional ways that it was generating new customers.

Avoid the "Shiny Object" Traffic Trap

Here's the other side of the coin: jumping from one source of traffic to another every week and never giving any of them enough time to work.

That's just as bad as relying on one thing.

The goal isn't to be *everywhere*. It's to **build a strong core**, then expand with intention.

Start with one or two sources that fit your business model.
Then build out additional layers as your funnel and messaging get dialed in.

Your Action Step

Ask yourself this:

- Where is 80% of my traffic coming from right now?
- What happens to my business if that source disappears tomorrow?
- What other channels could I test without overwhelming myself?
- Is my email list growing, or am I dependent on rented traffic?

Then pick one new channel to explore *and* one way to improve what you already have. Don't wait for the traffic rug to get pulled out. Start building a broader foundation now.

Bottom line?

Depending on one traffic source is like building a bridge with one support beam. It works… until it doesn't.

Diversify. Spread the risk. And make sure your business doesn't collapse when the traffic tides shift.

Chapter 26: Ignoring Organic Traffic and SEO Basics

If the word "SEO" makes your eyes glaze over, you're not alone.

For a lot of online business owners, it feels like some mysterious, overly technical world reserved for bloggers and big companies with marketing teams.

But here's the truth:

> **If you're ignoring organic traffic and SEO, you're ignoring one of the most powerful, long-term traffic sources your business can have.**

And even worse? You're probably missing out on customers who are *actively* searching for exactly what you offer.

Let that sink in: they're already looking for help. You're just not showing up.

What Is Organic Traffic, Anyway?

Organic traffic is the free stuff. It's people finding your content through Google, YouTube, or even Pinterest, without you paying for ads.

It takes longer to build than paid traffic. It's not instant. But when it kicks in? It pays off *over and over again.*

Think of it like planting seeds. You won't see results tomorrow, but in a few months, you've got something growing that doesn't need constant watering (or ad spend).

But SEO Is Too Complicated… Right?

It doesn't have to be.

You don't need to be an expert. You just need to get the **basics right.**

Things like:

- Knowing what your audience is searching for
- Writing pages and posts that clearly answer those questions
- Using relevant keywords in your headlines, subheads, and page descriptions
- Making sure your site loads fast and looks great on mobile
- Having clear internal links and a clean site structure

Most of this isn't even technical. It's just good content strategy and smart formatting.

Small Tweaks Can Bring Big Wins

Frank had a client who had great content, but zero SEO structure.

She had no headings, no meta descriptions, and her blog post titles were vague (think: "Thoughts on Tuesday" instead of "How to Save Time on Client Onboarding").

They optimized just a few posts. Cleaned up URLs. Added some relevant keywords. Renamed titles to match what people were searching for.

Within 30 days, she started seeing traffic from Google. Within 90 days, her best-performing blog post was bringing in daily leads, on autopilot.

That's the power of organic traffic. It keeps working long after you've stopped touching it.

Why You Can't Rely on Social Alone

Unlike social media posts that disappear in 24 hours, a solid piece of SEO content sticks around.

You post something valuable today, and Google can send traffic to it *next week, next month, even next year.*

That's leverage.

And it's the kind of leverage that compounds, especially if you're building your email list off the back of that content.

Your Action Step

Start simple. Pick one page or blog post to optimize this week.

- Research what your audience is typing into Google (use a tool like Ubersuggest, AnswerThePublic, or Google's "People Also Ask" section)
- Rewrite your headline to match one of those search terms
- Add a clear meta description (the short summary that shows up in Google)
- Break your content into sections with headings (use H2 and H3 tags)
- Link to other pages or blog posts on your site to keep people moving

If you don't have a blog yet, no problem, start with your homepage, about page, or FAQ page. All of it can be SEO-optimized.

Bottom line?

Ignoring SEO won't hurt you today. But in 6 months, you'll wish you'd started yesterday. Plant those seeds now. Learn the basics. And start building traffic you don't have to pay for, over and over again.

Chapter 27: Running Ads Without Understanding the Numbers

Running ads can feel exciting. You launch a campaign, throw some dollars at it, and wait for the magic to happen.

But here's the reality check:

> **If you don't understand the numbers, you're not running ads, you're just burning money.**

Facebook, Google, YouTube, they're all happy to take your money. But they're not going to tell you if your ad makes sense. That's *your* job.

And if you're just "boosting posts" or clicking the green button without tracking what's really happening?

That's not advertising. That's gambling.

You Don't Need to Be a Data Scientist… But You Do Need to Know the Basics

We're not saying you need to memorize your click-through rate down to the third decimal place.

But if you can't answer questions like:

- How much am I paying per lead?
- What's my conversion rate from click to customer?
- How much is a customer worth to me over time?

...then your ads are flying blind.

Because here's the deal: **running a profitable ad campaign isn't just about traffic. It's about *math*.**

The Numbers That Matter

There are a ton of metrics you can obsess over, but here are the big ones that actually affect your bottom line:

- **Cost Per Click (CPC):** What does it cost to get someone to your page?
- **Cost Per Lead (CPL):** What are you paying to get someone on your email list?
- **Conversion Rate:** Out of 100 people who hit your landing page, how many take action?
- **Customer Acquisition Cost (CAC):** How much does it take to get a buyer?
- **Customer Lifetime Value (CLTV):** What's the average value of a customer over time?

If you don't know these, it's nearly impossible to know whether your ads are working or just "feeling good."

We've Seen Businesses Sink Because They Didn't Know their Numbers

A guy Frank worked with was spending $100/day on Facebook ads. He was getting clicks and even some sales, but he didn't know how much each lead was costing or what each customer was worth.

After they ran the numbers?

He was spending $45 to acquire a $27 customer. Do that long enough and, well… you run out of money.

They paused the campaign, restructured his funnel, and raised prices on his backend. Same ads. Better results. Now he knew how to scale *profitably*, not just "get traffic."

Ads Without Tracking Is Like Flying Without Instruments

Would you get on a plane if the pilot said,

> "We don't have a speedometer or fuel gauge but we're gonna take off anyway and hope for the best!"?

Of course not. But that's what people do with ads daily.

They throw out money hoping for sales, but they don't track the journey. And that's why they think "ads don't work."

Ads *do* work when you know how to measure them.

Your Action Step

Before you spend another dollar on ads, get these things in place:

1. A clear **goal** (e.g., opt-ins, webinar signups, purchases)
2. A **tracking system** (Google Analytics, Facebook Pixel, or your ad platform dashboard)
3. A simple spreadsheet to track:
    - Ad spend
    - Clicks
    - Leads
    - Conversions
    - Revenue

Even if you're not a "numbers person," it doesn't need to be complicated. Track what's going in... and coming out. Once you do? Everything gets easier.

You can test headlines, tweak landing pages, scale what works, and kill what doesn't, *without guessing.*

Bottom line?

Running ads without tracking is like setting fire to your budget and hoping something good happens. Know your numbers. Learn the language of metrics. And turn your ad spend into *smart* spend.

Chapter 28: Not Following Up with Leads or Past Customers

Do you know what's easier than getting new leads?

Following up with the ones you already have.

Seriously. You've already spent the time, energy, or ad dollars to get someone's attention. Maybe they joined your email list, booked a call, or even bought something from you in the past.

But then what?

Crickets. Silence. You move on. They move on. And you leave money sitting on the table.

"They'll Reach Out If They Need Me…"

No, they won't. People are busy. They forget. They get distracted. Even if they *want* to buy from you again, they probably won't unless you show up in front of them, *again.*

Not following up doesn't feel like a big mistake, until you realize it's the difference between a one-time sale… and a business that grows.

And here's the wild part: some people are just waiting for a little nudge. A reminder. A follow-up email. A "Hey, are you still interested?" message.

That's all it takes.

The Fortune *Is* in the Follow-Up

We know it's a cliché. But clichés stick around because they're true. Following up with leads and past customers isn't about being pushy, it's about being *present*.

It's about continuing the relationship.

- Someone downloads your lead magnet?
  Follow up.
- Someone books a call but doesn't buy?
  Follow up.
- Someone buys once and never again? Follow up.

You'd be shocked how many people will say "yes" on the second or third ask, *if* you ask.

Why We Avoid It (And Why That's a Problem)

Let's be honest: most of us avoid follow-up for a few reasons:

- We're scared of being annoying.

- We think if they didn't buy the first time, they never will.
- We're too busy chasing *new* leads to circle back on old ones.

But here's the truth:

> **The easiest sale to make is to someone who already knows you.**

They've seen your brand. They've heard your voice. They already trust you, at least a little.

You just have to re-engage the conversation.

We've Seen Clients Double Sales with One Follow-Up

A client had a list of over 1,000 people who downloaded a lead magnet over the past year… and never heard from him again.

We wrote a simple 3-email sequence:

- Email 1: "Still interested in [topic]?"
- Email 2: Value-packed tip
- Email 3: Soft offer with a clear next step

Result? 11 new clients in 10 days. No ad spend. No extra traffic. Just follow-up.

Your Action Step

Start simple. Ask yourself:

- Who hasn't heard from me in a while?
- What can I send them that adds value and reopens the conversation?
- What's one clear action I want them to take?

Then write one email. Send it today. And watch what happens. You don't need a 30-day campaign, just a willingness to reconnect.

Also, set up automation where it makes sense.

- Opt-in? Follow up automatically.
- Sale? Deliver, then ask for the next step.
- No purchase yet? Stay in touch with helpful content.

Bottom line?

If you're not following up, you're not just missing out, you're *giving up* on people who've already said they're interested.

Don't do that. Follow up. Stay connected. And watch how many "maybes" turn into "yes."

Chapter 29: Using Confusing or Generic Copy Instead of Direct, Benefit-Driven Language

We've all seen it...

Websites full of phrases like:

> "We empower individuals through innovative solutions."
> "Helping you achieve your goals with cutting-edge tools."
> "Our mission is to deliver value through transformational strategy."

Sounds fancy, right? Except... what does any of that actually *mean*?

Spoiler alert:

If your visitors have to work to figure out what you do, they won't stick around to figure it out.

Clarity Beats Clever,
Every Time

It's tempting to write copy that sounds impressive. Corporate. "Professional." But the truth is, **most people**

don't want clever. They want clear.

They want to know *what you do*, *how it helps them*, and *why they should care*, and they want to know it fast.

Because they're not reading your site like a novel. They're skimming. Looking for the one thing that tells them, *"Yep, this is for me."*

If they don't find it? They're gone.

Why Generic Copy Doesn't Convert

Generic copy tries to speak to everyone… and ends up connecting with no one. It lacks urgency. It lacks emotion. It lacks direction.

It doesn't paint a picture. It doesn't solve a problem. And most importantly, it doesn't answer the golden question:

"What's in it for me?"

People don't care how smart you sound. They care how you can help them *solve their problem or reach their goal*.

What Direct, Benefit-Driven Copy Looks Like

Let's say you help small businesses with bookkeeping.

You could say:

> "We provide accounting solutions to help streamline your operations."

Or you could say:

> **"We help small business owners stop stressing over spreadsheets and finally feel confident about their cash flow."**

One sounds like a brochure. The other sounds like you understand their pain, and know how to fix it.

Benefit-driven copy:

- Speaks to a specific pain or desire
- Uses simple, everyday language
- Focuses on *outcomes*, not features
- Tells the reader what's in it for them

Rewriting Copy Can Change the Game

Frank once helped a client revise the headline on their homepage. It originally said:

> "Providing Solutions for Digital Success."

They changed it to:

> **"Get a Website That Actually Converts Visitors Into Customers."**

That one tweak? Increased opt-ins by 40%. No new design. No new product. Just clearer language.

That's the power of dialing in your copy.

Your Action Step

Do a quick copy audit.

Start with your homepage, sales page, or lead magnet landing page and ask:

- Is it immediately clear *who this is for* and *what it does*?
- Are you speaking in benefits ("save time," "grow your income") or just listing features?
- Could a stranger land on your site and *instantly* know why they should care?

If not, rewrite. Simplify. Add clarity. Make the message punchier. One line at a time.

Bottom line?

Confusing or generic copy kills conversions. Clear, benefit-driven language builds trust, attention, and action.

So stop trying to sound impressive. Start sounding *helpful*.

Tell people what they'll get. Tell them how it helps. And tell them exactly what to do next.

Chapter 30: Forgetting the Power of Testimonials and Reviews

Here's something you already know, but probably aren't using enough:

People believe other people more than they believe you.

You can have the best copy in the world. A killer offer. A beautiful site. But nothing beats the power of a real person saying, **"This worked for me."**

That's why forgetting to collect and use testimonials is such a costly mistake. It's like leaving free sales ammo on the table.

Social Proof Is the Secret Sauce

We live in a world where people check Amazon reviews before buying a $10 phone charger. So, if you're selling a service, a product, or a course, and you don't have **clear, authentic testimonials** front and center, you're already behind.

It's not about bragging. It's about *trust*.

A good testimonial tells your potential customer:

> "You're not the first. You're not the guinea
> pig. And this isn't a scam."

It validates your claims. It reduces risk. It's proof that real people got real results.

"But I Don't Have Any Testimonials Yet..."

Sure you do.

If you've ever helped someone, paid or unpaid, you've got a starting point. Ask them for a sentence or two. Offer to write it for them and let them approve it.

Even if you're brand new, you can give away your product or service to 3–5 people in exchange for honest feedback. Not only will you get testimonials, you'll also get insights that can help improve what you offer.

Pro tip: when asking for testimonials, don't just say,

> "Can you write something nice?"

Ask specific questions like:

- What was your biggest challenge before working with me?
- What made you choose this product/service?
- What results did you get?
- How would you describe the experience?

These questions lead to testimonials that tell a *story*, not just fluff.

Testimonials Have Doubled Conversions

Frank helped a client relaunch a sales page that was performing okay, but not great.

They didn't change the product. They didn't rewrite the copy. They simply added three clear, results-driven testimonials above the call-to-action and two more throughout the page.

Conversions doubled. Why? Because people saw themselves in those stories. They felt reassured. They stopped wondering "Will this work for me?", and started saying, "Looks like it worked for them... maybe it'll work for me too."

That's the power of proof.

Where to Use Testimonials

Once you've got good testimonials, don't hide them. Use them strategically:

- On your homepage.
- On your sales pages.
- In your email funnels.
- In your lead magnets.
- On checkout pages.

- In retargeting ads.
- On social posts.

Don't just have a "Testimonials" tab on your menu. That's where testimonials go to die. Sprinkle them throughout your site, **right where people need reassurance.**

Your Action Step

Make a list of your happy clients, customers, or students. Reach out to 5 of them today. Ask for short, honest feedback using the prompt questions above.

Already have testimonials? Revisit them.

- Are they too vague? ("Great service!" doesn't work)
- Do they mention the results?
- Do they speak to common objections or fears?
- Are they in the right spots on your site?

Update, organize, and put them to work.

Bottom line?

You can say you're great all day long. But when *someone else* says it? That's when trust gets built, and sales start happening. So, stop leaving social proof in the inbox. Put it front and center where it belongs.

P.S. Want to see a suggested format for testimonials? Check out Bret's page at https://BretRidgway.com/rave-reviews

Product & Offer Mistakes

You can have the perfect website... a solid marketing plan... even traffic rolling in like clockwork.

But if your **product or offer isn't dialed in**, none of that matters.

This section is all about the big mistakes online business owners make when it comes to *what* they're selling and *how* they're selling it.

From pricing too low to offering too much (or too little), we'll break down the costly missteps that sabotage your sales and stall your growth.

Because here's the truth:

People don't buy products, they buy outcomes. If your offer doesn't clearly deliver value, results, and confidence, they're gone.

Don't worry, we're going to fix that.

Let's dive into the offer mistakes that might be holding you back (and show you how to fix them fast).

Chapter 31: Creating a Product Without Validating Demand

Let's just call this what it is:

One of the most expensive mistakes you can make in your online business.

You get excited. You spend weeks, maybe months, building the "perfect" course, service, membership, or digital product.

You polish every detail. Record the videos. Design the funnel. And when it's finally done, you hit publish and wait for the flood of sales to roll in.

But what happens?

Crickets.

A few clicks, maybe. A pity sale from your cousin. But no real traction. Not because your product was bad, but because you skipped the most important step:

You didn't validate the demand.

Don't Build in a Vacuum

Here's the truth: Just because *you* think it's a great idea doesn't mean the market does.

The internet isn't short on content. It's short on relevance. If your product doesn't solve a *real, urgent, painful problem* for a specific group of people, it doesn't matter how good it is.

That's why validation matters. Because it tells you:

- Is this something people really want?
- Will they pay for it?
- How are they talking about the problem?
- What alternatives are they already using?

Without those answers, you're building blind.

Validation Doesn't Mean Perfection

You don't need a massive research report or a 3-month survey. Sometimes, validation is as simple as:

- Posting an idea on social and seeing who engages

- Sending an email with a soft pitch and tracking interest

- Pre-selling access to a beta version

- Interviewing 5–10 people in your target audience

- Looking at competitors and customer reviews

You're not asking for compliments, you're looking for *patterns*. Are people already spending money to fix this problem? Do they say things like, "I've been looking for something like this"?

We've Both Built Things Nobody Bought

Yep, been there.

Years ago Bret created a course he *knew* was going to crush. He poured everything into it. But he made one big mistake: he never asked anyone if they *wanted* it.

Launched it to his list... and it flopped.

Why? Because he built what he thought they needed, not what they *actually* wanted. He was solving a problem they didn't think they had.

Lesson learned.

Now he starts by asking questions. He tests the waters. If he doesn't get a strong signal of interest? He pivots, or he waits.

Your Product Isn't Just an Idea, It's a Conversation

The best products come from listening. Pay attention to:

- The questions your audience asks.
- The problems they complain about.
- The phrases they repeat.
- The content that gets the most engagement.

That's where your next offer should come from, not just what you feel like building.

When you create from *demand*, sales get easier. When you create from *assumptions*, they often don't happen at all.

Your Action Step

Before you build another offer, validate it:

1. Write a one-paragraph description of the product idea.
2. Send it to your list or post it to your audience with a call-to-action (e.g., "Would you be interested in this?" or "Want early access?").
3. Track responses, and pay attention to *enthusiasm*, not just politeness.
4. If you get good feedback, offer a simple preorder, waitlist, or beta sign-up.
5. Build *only* when you know people are ready to buy.

This saves you time. It protects your energy. And it keeps your business focused on what people *actually want.*

Bottom line?

Don't build in the dark and hope for a sale. Shine a light on demand first, and let the market guide your next move.

Because the best product in the world means nothing... if nobody wants to buy it.

A footnote to this chapter

Many years ago Bret founded the first website in the plant engineering and maintenance industry. On that site he featured some free resources and also sold products aimed at plant engineers, maintenance mechanics, electricians, pipefitters and other skilled trades people.

The products sold included books, training materials, training equipment, videotapes (remember VHS tapes?), and more. He compiled a robust catalog of products to sell by making distribution agreements with dozens of technical publishers and other companies who offered products within that niche.

As a distributor Bret typically received anywhere from a 20% to 40% profit margin when a product was sold. So, a $100 sale resulted in $20 to $40 going into Bret's pocket.

Well, when he factored in all the overhead expenses associated with running that online business he found it was tough to make much of a profit after all was said and done. Most products also had to be inventoried, so there was a continual outlay of capital to keep products in stock.

That's why we feel it is critical for your long-term success to be selling your own products as much as possible. You need to have products where you receive 100% of the sales price, not just 20-40%.

Now, some people can do quite well with what is known as affiliate marketing. Selling other people's products can be profitable if (and it's a big if) you have your own email list to sell to. But generally, it's those products that you have created yourself and that you receive all the proceeds of the sale for that will lead to the greatest chance of online success.

Chapter 32: Offering Too Many Products/Services at Once

When you're passionate, skilled, and full of ideas, it's easy to think...

"I'll offer it all. More options mean more sales, right?"

Wrong.

In fact, offering too many products or services at once is one of the fastest ways to stall your business and confuse your customers.

Because here's what most people don't realize:

A confused visitor never becomes a customer.

Too Much Choice = Decision Paralysis

We've all seen it:

You land on a website and there are 14 different offers. Courses, coaching, templates, a membership, three free PDFs, a done-for-you service, a group program, and a bonus one-on-one strategy call (only available Tuesdays at noon).

Instead of saying, *"Yes, I want this!"* You end up thinking, *"I'll come back later."*

Spoiler: they don't.

People aren't looking for a buffet. They're looking for a *clear path.* And when everything is important, *nothing* feels important.

More Offers = More Stress (for You)

It's not just confusing for your audience, it's exhausting for *you.*

Each product needs:

- Its own messaging
- Its own sales funnel
- Its own delivery system
- Its own follow-up
- Its own customer support

Multiply that by 3, 4, or 5 products, and you've just built yourself a full-time job managing complexity... instead of growing a streamlined business.

Trust me, we've been there.

Years ago, we each had multiple courses, coaching tiers, templates, and toolkits... all live at once. It looked impressive from the outside, but behind the scenes?

It was chaos. Too much to manage, too many moving parts, and not enough sales from *any* of it to make it worth the energy.

The Power of Focus

Want to grow faster?

Simplify.

Focus on **one core offer** that solves a clear, painful problem for a specific audience. Build around that. Refine it. Test it. Learn what your customers need next, and then *layer* on additional offers over time.

When you build one winning offer, you gain momentum. When you try to juggle five at once, everything suffers.

We've Seen Businesses Transform by Cutting Back

Frank had a coaching client with six different services on their homepage. They cut it down to *one package*, with three tiers (starter, standard, premium). Same skills. Same delivery. Just simplified.

Sales jumped. Why? Because now visitors knew exactly what to buy.

That's what clarity does.

Your Action Step

Take inventory of your current offers:

- Which one brings in the most revenue?
- Which one is easiest to deliver?
- Which one are you *most* excited to sell?

That's your core offer.

Focus on it. Promote it. Build your funnel around it. Let the others go, or park them for later.

When your audience knows exactly what you offer, why it matters, and how to take the next step, *sales happen faster.*

Bottom line?

You don't need more offers. You need one great offer with a clear message and a smooth path to buy.

So simplify. Streamline. And let your business grow with *focus*, not frenzy.

Chapter 33: Undervaluing What You Sell (Pricing Too Low)

Let's talk about pricing and the fear that comes with it.

You've created something solid. You've helped people. You've seen the results. And yet, when it's time to put a price tag on it... you freeze.

You start thinking:

> "What if it's too expensive?"
> "Will anyone actually pay this?"
> "Maybe I'll keep it low to get more buyers..."

So you price it safe. You price it low. And you end up working twice as hard for half the reward.

Here's the truth:

> **If you don't value what you sell, neither will anyone else.**

Low Prices Don't Build Confidence, They Raise Red Flags

We like to think lower prices will attract more customers. And maybe at first, they do. But in the long run? They *undermine your value.*

Because price isn't just a number, it's a signal.

- A $27 course says, "This is a quick tip."
- A $270 course says, "This goes deeper."
- A $2,700 program says, "This will change your life."

When you price too low, people assume your product is basic... or incomplete... or amateur.

Not because it is, but because that's what the price *says*.

Cheap Customers = Expensive Headaches

There's another side to this, too.

Low-ticket buyers tend to be:

- Needier
- Less committed
- More likely to ask for refunds
- More likely to ghost you after buying

Meanwhile, higher-paying customers show up. They pay attention. They respect your time. And they *value the outcome.*

We've seen it over and over again.

Frank had a client who doubled the price of her coaching package, and ended up with fewer clients, *more revenue,* and a whole lot less stress.

The Real Problem: Fear of Rejection

Let's be honest: most pricing issues aren't about math. They're about mindset.

We're scared that if we raise our prices:

- People will say no
- We'll lose sales
- We'll look arrogant
- We won't feel "worth it"

But here's the flip side:

> **When you price confidently, the right people pay attention.**

They're not buying based on what it costs. They're buying based on what it's *worth*, to them.

When you can clearly communicate the transformation or result you deliver, *value-based pricing* makes total sense.

We've Raised Prices and Watched Sales Go Up

There was a time when we both undercharged for everything. Websites, coaching, courses, you name it. We were afraid to raise our rates.

But as we got better results for clients and built track records, we realized: '**We weren't just selling "a thing." We were selling outcomes.**

And those outcomes were worth more than we were charging.

So, we raised our prices. Not overnight, but steadily. And you know what happened?

- We attracted better clients.
- We closed more sales (with less effort).
- And people *trusted us more* because our pricing matched our expertise.

Your Action Step

Ask yourself:

- What is the *transformation* my product or service delivers?
- What is that transformation *worth* to the customer in dollars, time, or peace of mind?
- Am I pricing based on what it costs me to deliver… or on what it's worth to them?

Then do this:

- Raise your prices, even just by 10–20%.
- Update your messaging to reflect the *value*, not just the features.

- Add testimonials, guarantees, or bonuses that support that price point.

You'll be amazed at what happens when you start charging what you're truly worth.

Bottom line?

If you keep undervaluing your offer, the market will follow your lead.

So, stop apologizing for your prices. Start owning the value you deliver, and charge accordingly.

Because confidence sells. And underpricing is one mistake that costs more than you think.

Chapter 34: No Guarantee or Risk Reversal

Let's talk trust.

Because no matter how good your offer is, if someone's never bought from you before, they're wondering one thing:

"What if this doesn't work for me?"

That little voice in their head? It's whispering worst-case scenarios:

- What if I waste my money?
- What if I don't get results?
- What if it's not what I expected?
- What if this person disappears after I buy?

And if you don't address that fear head-on, you're leaving them to wrestle with it alone.

That's where a guarantee, or a smart risk reversal, can turn "I'm not sure" into "Let's do this."

Why Guarantees Aren't Optional

A guarantee isn't just a refund policy. It's a **confidence signal**.

It says, "I believe in this enough to take the risk off of you and put it on me."

And when you do that, people *relax*. Their defenses come down. They feel safe enough to say yes.

Think about it: we buy from Amazon with confidence not just because it's convenient, but because we know we can return something if it doesn't fit or function.

That same principle works for your business, whether you sell coaching, courses, software, or services.

"But Won't People Abuse It?"

Look, there's always going to be that one person. But they're the exception, not the rule.

Most people are honest. And here's what we've seen, time and again:

> **The more confident your guarantee, the fewer refunds you actually get.**

It's a paradox, but it's true.

Because the people who are going to buy, use, and *value* your product are reassured by your confidence. And the tire-kickers? They'll hesitate no matter what you do.

What Kind of Guarantee Should You Offer?

There's no one-size-fits-all, but here are a few solid options:

- **30-Day No Questions Asked Refund** – Great for digital products or courses.

- **Satisfaction Guarantee** – "If you're not happy, neither am I. Let me fix it or give your money back."

- **Try It, Love It, Or Leave It** – Adds personality and approachability.

- **Results-Based Guarantee** – "If you follow the steps and don't see results, I'll work with you until you do, or give a refund."

The goal isn't just to *protect* the customer, it's to *remove the fear.*

Even better? Put your guarantee near the buy button, in your checkout area, and mention it in your sales emails. Let it be part of the decision process, not fine print.

We've Seen a Simple Guarantee Boost Conversions Instantly

One client had a course priced at $497. Solid value, great content, but low conversion.

We added a "100% satisfaction or your money back within 30 days" guarantee, along with a short video of her explaining it personally.

Sales increased by over 30%. Nothing else changed.

Why? Because that one tweak addressed the one thing her audience was silently unsure about: *"What if it's not worth it?"*

She answered that question with confidence and got rewarded for it.

Your Action Step

Ask yourself:

- Where can I add or strengthen a guarantee in my funnel?
- What's the biggest risk my audience *feels*, and how can I reverse it?
- Can I give a refund, a swap, extra support, or a commitment that makes them feel secure?

Then write your guarantee in plain, friendly language. No legalese. No tricks.

Make it human. Make it bold. And stand behind it.

Bottom line?

When you remove the risk, you remove resistance.

So stop making your customers shoulder all the uncertainty. Step up. Offer the guarantee. And watch your conversions rise.

Because people don't need more pressure. They need more *confidence.*

Chapter 35: Not Clearly Explaining the Transformation or Result

Let's make this simple:

People don't buy products. They buy outcomes.

Nobody wakes up thinking, *"I hope I find a new course today."*

What they're really thinking is:

- "I need to finally get control of my business."
- "I want to stop feeling overwhelmed."
- "I need to make more money."
- "I want to feel confident doing this myself."

If your copy, sales page, or pitch doesn't speak directly to that transformation, they're gone.

What's In It for Me?

That's the question running through every visitor's head.
And if they don't get a clear, fast answer? They bounce.

Too many entrepreneurs talk about what their product *is* instead of what it *does*.

> **"Includes 7 video modules, PDF worksheets, and a 60-minute bonus call!"**

Okay… but what's the result?

> **"Learn how to double your lead conversions in 30 days, without spending a dime on ads."**

Now we're talking.

Because that's not just a product. That's a *promise*.

Features Tell. Results Sell.

You might be proud of how much you packed into your offer, and you should be! But your prospect isn't looking for a syllabus. They're looking for a *solution*.

They want to know:

- What will change in their life or business after they use it?
- How will it make things easier, faster, cheaper, or more fulfilling?
- What problem will finally go away?
- What dream will finally feel within reach?

If you don't tell them… they won't guess.

Sales Pages Can Turn Around with One Sentence

A client came to Frank with a beautiful-looking offer. It had all the pieces: testimonials, features, bonus stack, clean design.

But sales were flat.

The reason? It never clearly explained what the user *gets* out of the experience. Lots of "what's included," zero "what's in it for me."

They added one headline and two bullet points that nailed the transformation:

> "Go from struggling to sell your services...
> to confidently booking clients who pay what
> you're worth."

Boom. Instant connection. The message finally landed, and conversions followed.

Want to Sell More? Get Specific.

Don't just say, "You'll improve your mindset."

Say, "You'll wake up feeling in control of your day, instead of dreading your to-do list."

Don't say, "You'll learn about investing."

Say, "You'll walk away with a 3-step plan to grow your money, without guessing, gambling, or watching the market every day."

Paint a picture. Make it real. Speak to their now, and show them their *after*.

Your Action Step

Go look at your product page, your opt-in offer, your course description, anywhere you're trying to sell or get someone to take action.

Ask yourself:

- Is the transformation obvious in the first 10 seconds?
- Can someone skim and understand what problem it solves?
- Does it *feel* like a result they want?

If not, rework your headline and the first few lines of copy. Lead with the end result. Then back it up with how it works.

Bottom line?

If you don't explain the transformation clearly, you're asking people to buy in the dark.

Shine a light on the outcome. Show them what's waiting on the other side. And make your offer impossible to ignore.

Chapter 36: Assuming People Understand Your Offer Without Guidance

You've built something great. You've poured in time, effort, strategy, and maybe even sleepless nights.

And then... nothing.

People visit your sales page, your service menu, and maybe even your checkout. But they don't buy. Not because they aren't interested...

But because they don't *get it*.

> **One of the biggest mistakes you can make is assuming people understand what your offer is, and how to take the next step.**

If You Confuse, You Lose

This one hits hard because it's so easy to miss.

You know your offer like the back of your hand. You know what it includes, what it helps with, how it works, and why it's valuable.

But your audience? They're seeing it for the first time. They're not connecting dots. They're not reading between lines. They need **clarity, direction, and next steps, spelled out.**

Because if they're left guessing, they're not clicking "Buy Now." They're clicking away.

What This Looks Like in Real Life

Here's what we've seen over and over again:

- A sales page that uses insider language or vague benefits.

- A coaching offer that sounds like "support + strategy" but never explains *how* it works.

- A service menu with no clear call-to-action, just floating prices and bullet points.

- A product page with multiple buttons and no direction on *which* one to click.

- Checkout processes with zero guidance on what happens after purchase.

It's not that the offer is bad. It's that people don't know *what it is, how it works, or what to do next.*

"They'll Figure It Out…" No, They Won't.

Your job as the business owner isn't to sound smart, it's to be clear. You're the guide, not the gatekeeper. You're there to walk people through the decision, not leave them standing at the door wondering where to knock.

> **A confused prospect won't ask questions. They'll just disappear.**

The Fix: Spell It Out

Here's how you bring clarity to your offer:

- Tell them **exactly** what they're getting.
- Show them what happens **after** they buy.
- Explain **who it's for** and **who it's not for.**
- Give them a **single, clear call-to-action** (no "Learn More" *and* "Book Now" *and* "Subscribe Here" on the same page).
- Use plain language. Skip the jargon. Talk like a human.

And most of all? Guide them through the process like it's the first time they've ever heard of you, because it probably is.

You Can Turn Around an Offer Just by Adding Clarity

One client had a great program. She was getting tons of clicks to her page, but almost zero conversions.

When we looked at her sales page, we saw the issue right away:

- No explanation of how the offer worked
- No visuals or timelines.
- No mention of what happens after payment.
- Multiple buttons that led to different outcomes.

We rewrote it with step-by-step clarity, added a visual breakdown, and moved one button above the fold with a "Here's exactly what happens next" section.

Sales picked up immediately.

Because the product didn't need to change. The *understanding* did.

Your Action Step

Audit your offer page, right now.

Ask yourself:

- Would a total stranger understand what I'm offering in 30 seconds or less?
- Do I clearly explain the process or delivery?
- Is there a single, obvious next step, and is it easy to take?

If not, tighten it up. Use simple visuals if needed. Walk them through it like they've never heard of your business before, because, for the most part, that's exactly the case.

Bottom line?

Don't assume they know what you know. Assume they're curious… but distracted, overwhelmed, and unsure.

Be the guide. Light the way. And you'll turn hesitation into confidence, and confidence into conversions.

Chapter 37: Ignoring Upsells, Downsells, and Recurring Revenue Opportunities

Let us put it bluntly:

> **If you're not offering an upsell, a downsell, or some kind of recurring income... you're leaving money on the table.**

And not just loose change, this is the kind of mistake that keeps you working way harder than you need to.

We get it. You finally got the sale. You're relieved. You're excited. But what most online business owners miss is this:

> The *easiest* time to make a second sale is **right after** the first one.

That's where upsells, downsells, and recurring offers come in. They're not "advanced strategies", they're common sense business growth tools that a lot of people overlook.

You've Seen It Before (And It Works)

You know how the drive-thru worker asks, *"Want fries with that?"* That's an upsell. And it's made fast food chains billions.

Same thing when Amazon shows you, *"Frequently bought together..."* They're stacking value and increasing the order total, *without* chasing a new customer.

Meanwhile, many entrepreneurs hustle their tails off to make one sale... and then stop. No follow-up. No add-on. No next step.

That's a mistake.

Let's Break It Down

- **Upsell:** A higher-priced or add-on product offered *after* the initial purchase. Think bonus modules, private coaching, or extra features.

- **Downsell:** A lower-priced alternative if the main offer feels too big. Like a self-study guide instead of a full coaching package.

- **Recurring revenue:** Ongoing income from subscriptions or retainers. Think memberships, software, monthly services, or support plans.

If you don't offer at least one of these in your business, you're relying way too much on *first-time buyers* to hit your goals.

Real Talk From Our World

There was a client years ago who launched a solid course. Great value, good price point, solid audience. He sold 100 copies at $97.

But there was nothing else, no upsell, no monthly group coaching, nothing beyond the initial course.

Compare that to another client in a similar niche. She sold her $97 course *with* a $47/month community add-on and a $197 upsell for a private call.

Her average customer value? Over $200. Same effort, more revenue, better customer support.

That's what a little strategy can do.

Why You Need This in Your Business

Here's what happens when you don't offer these things:

- You work harder just to break even.
- You get stuck in launch mode.
- You leave your best customers without a next step.
- You miss predictable, stable income.

On the flip side, when you *do* implement them, even in simple ways, you can:

- Increase profit per customer.
- Serve people more deeply.
- Stabilize your monthly income.
- Grow *without* burning out.

Your Action Step

Pick one offer you already have. Now ask:

- **What's one upsell?** (A VIP version? A done-for-you add-on?).
- **What's one downsell?** (A simpler, cheaper version?).
- **Is there a recurring element?** (Could I turn this into a monthly service, community, or support plan?).

Start with one. Add it to your checkout page, your thank you email, or even in a follow-up sequence.

It doesn't have to be fancy. It just has to be **offered**.

Bottom line?

If you're not giving your customers the chance to buy more or stay longer, you're short-changing them *and* your business.

Bret once had an offer of an audio interview with a colleague that was a low ticket item - like $17. A PDF transcript of the call was offered as an upsell at $27. A full 95% of buyers took advantage of the upsell.

So go ahead, ask if they want the fries. They might say yes.

Chapter 38: No Urgency or Scarcity in Promotions

Here's a question for you...

> When was the last time you bought something *without* any reason to buy it now?

Not often, right?

We wait. We think about it. We tell ourselves, *"I'll come back to it later."* And nine times out of ten... we don't.

Guess what? Your prospects do the same thing. And if your offer doesn't have a reason to act now, chances are, they won't.

No urgency = no movement
No scarcity = no decision

People Don't Just Buy What You Sell, They Buy *When* You Sell It

The difference between a trickle of sales and a flood of orders often comes down to one thing: **A compelling reason to act.**

Urgency and scarcity aren't sleazy tactics. They're decision-making tools. They help people move from *thinking* to *doing.*

Because even when someone *wants* what you offer… if they don't have a reason to pull the trigger *today,* they'll wait. And waiting turns into forgetting.

So, What Does Urgency Look Like?

Urgency is time-based. It says:

> "This won't be around forever."

Examples include:

- A deadline: "Doors close Friday at midnight."
- A countdown: "Only 48 hours left."
- A seasonal window: "Only open for Black Friday."
- A timed bonus: "Register in the next 24 hours and get the bonus package."

Urgency pushes people to decide now, not later.

What About Scarcity?

Scarcity is quantity-based. It says:

> "This isn't available to everyone."

Examples:

- "Only 100 seats available."
- "We're only taking 10 clients this month."
- "Limited edition, once it's gone, it's gone."
- "3 spots left on the group coaching call."

Scarcity increases perceived value and reduces procrastination. People act fast when they know something's about to run out.

We've Watched These Elements Double (and Triple) Conversions

Once helped a client relaunch a digital course that wasn't converting well.

We added:

- A 5-day launch window (urgency).
- A fast-action bonus for the first 20 buyers (scarcity).
- Clear countdown timers on the page and emails.

Same product. Same price. Same audience.

Result? Triple the sales.

Because now buyers had a reason to say yes *now*, instead of "maybe later."

But Isn't That Manipulative?

Not if you're honest. There's a big difference between fake scarcity ("Only 3 left!" when it's a digital product with infinite access) and **real, ethical urgency.**

You're not tricking people, you're helping them decide. And let's face it: we all need a little nudge sometimes.

Your Action Step

Look at your next promo, offer, or email sequence and ask:

- **Where's the urgency?** (Is there a real deadline?).
- **Where's the scarcity?** (Is there a cap, a bonus, or limited availability?).
- **Am I communicating this clearly?** (Is it visible, repeated, and believable?).

Add one real urgency trigger and one scarcity trigger to your next campaign. You'll see people move faster. Decide quicker. And buy while the offer's hot.

Bottom line?

If there's no reason to act now, most people won't.

So give them a reason. Set a timer. Limit a bonus. And watch your sales start moving.

Chapter 39: Forgetting to Ask for the Sale (Being Too Passive)

You've seen it, and maybe you've done it too.

You create a great offer. You write value-packed emails. You publish helpful content. You share testimonials, benefits, and features.

But then... silence.

Why? Because you never actually **asked** for the sale.

> **Being helpful is great. Being passive is not.**

Here's the harsh truth: If you don't confidently ask people to take the next step, they probably won't.

Hinting Isn't Selling

"I hope you'll consider..."
"If this sounds like something you might like..."
"Feel free to reach out if you have questions..."

Those aren't calls to action. Those are *invitations to keep scrolling.*

Your audience isn't going to stop and think, *"Wait, is this the part where I'm supposed to buy?"*

You have to **tell them**.

Be clear. Be confident. Be direct.

If your offer helps people, it's not pushy, it's a *disservice* not to make it clear how they can get it.

What Asking Looks Like

You don't need high-pressure tactics or flashing "BUY NOW" buttons on every page.

You just need a simple, clear statement:

- "Click here to get started."
- "Let's book your call now."
- "Buy the course and get instant access."
- "Grab your spot before the doors close."

Whatever it is, make the next step **crystal clear** and repeat it. People want guidance. Give it to them.

The Confidence Gap

Let's be real: most people who avoid asking for the sale aren't lazy... they're unsure.

- *What if they say no?*
- *What if I sound pushy?*
- *What if I'm not ready?*

But remember, **you're not selling snake oil.**

If you've built something valuable that solves a real problem, your job is to lead people to it, not leave them guessing.

Confidence doesn't mean hype. It means **standing behind your offer** and inviting people to take action with zero hesitation.

One Call to Action (CTA) Can Change Everything

Once had a client with a sales page that had great content, but no strong CTA until the very bottom, and even that was just a soft "learn more" button.

We added three bold, benefit-focused calls to action:

- One above the fold.
- One after the first testimonial.
- One at the end, right after the offer recap.

Sales jumped. Not because the offer changed. Because the **invitation got clearer**.

Your Action Step

Check your sales page, email, or lead magnet and ask:

- **Did I clearly tell them what to do next?**

- **Is there a button or link within view at every scroll point?**
- **Am I asking like I believe in it, or like I'm apologizing for it?**

Then rewrite one weak call to action today. Make it clear. Make it confident. Make it count.

Bottom line?

Don't hope people will "figure it out." Don't whisper your offer from the back of the room.

Step up. Ask for the sale. And guide people confidently to the solution you created for them.

Chapter 40: Never Updating or Improving the Product Based on Feedback

You finally launch your product. People buy it. You breathe a sigh of relief and think, *"Whew, I'm done!"*

But here's the problem:

Done is never really done.

Products, like businesses, need to evolve. And if you're not listening, updating, or improving based on customer feedback, you're not just standing still, you're falling behind.

Feedback Isn't Criticism, It's Fuel

A lot of business owners avoid feedback because they're scared of what they might hear.

- *What if someone doesn't like it?*
- *What if I missed something?*
- *What if it's not as good as I thought?*

Here's the thing: **that's how you get better.**

Customer feedback isn't an attack. It's insight. It tells you what's working, what's unclear, and what could take your offer from "pretty good" to "can't live without it."

Great Products Can Get Left Behind

Years ago, Frank bought a solid piece of software from a solo developer. Worked great. Solved a real problem. He recommended it to everyone.

But six months later… nothing had changed. The bugs weren't fixed. Features people asked for never came. The interface still looked like 2003.

People stopped using it. He stopped recommending it. Not because it wasn't useful, because it **wasn't evolving.**

Meanwhile, a competitor came in, listened to user feedback, launched updates every month, and won the market.

Your First Version Isn't Your Final Version

Even if your launch goes great, even if the testimonials roll in, you're not done. You've just begun.

Ask yourself:

- Are you regularly checking in with customers post-purchase?
- Do you have a way to collect and organize feedback?
- Are you tracking support tickets or refund requests for patterns?

Every question, complaint, or suggestion is a free roadmap.

Listen to your customers. They'll tell you what to fix, what to expand, and what to drop.

Simple Ways to Stay Ahead

You don't need a fancy feedback system. You just need to pay attention.

- Add a short survey after someone completes your course or uses your service.
- Ask: "What was most helpful?" and "What could be better?"
- Track recurring questions in your support inbox.
- Run a "version 2.0" update and announce it as a bonus to your existing buyers.
- Release new modules, bonus templates, or revised lessons over time.

These small touches show your audience that you care, and they increase trust, loyalty, and repeat sales.

Your Action Step

Take one of your current products, course, service, software, anything, and ask:

- **When was the last time I updated it?**
- **What feedback have I gotten that I haven't acted on?**
- **What's one improvement I could make this week?**

Even a small update, like adding a bonus video or tightening a lesson, can make a big difference in perceived value.

Then tell your audience. Let them know you're listening, learning, and improving.

Bottom line?

Your product isn't a one-and-done project. It's a living asset. if you're not improving it, someone else is improving theirs.

So keep listening. Keep leveling up. Show your customers that you don't just want their money, you want their success.

Email & Communication Mistakes

You've probably heard that "the money's in the list." And it's true, **but only if you actually communicate with that list.**

This section dives into the mistakes business owners make when it comes to emails, follow-ups, and messaging, the kind of missteps that quietly kill trust, tank conversions, and leave your audience cold.

Because here's the deal:

> Your email list isn't just a bunch of names.
> It's a conversation waiting to happen.

If you're ghosting your subscribers, sending boring broadcasts, or writing emails that feel like spam instead of value... you're missing out on one of the most powerful tools in your online business.

Let's fix that.

Chapter 41: Not Emailing Your List Regularly

Let's just rip the Band-Aid off:

> If you're not emailing your list consistently,
> you're leaving money, and relationships, on
> the table.

You worked hard to build that list. You created a lead magnet. You got people to subscribe. And then... nothing?

Weeks go by. Maybe months. And suddenly, your list goes from *interested audience* to *total strangers*.

Out of Sight, Out of Inbox

People's inboxes are noisy. You're not the only one competing for their attention. If you're not showing up regularly, they forget who you are.

And when you *do* finally send an email, maybe to promote your new offer, it feels random. Cold. Out of place.

> You're not just fighting for attention... now
> you're fighting to be remembered.

"The single biggest problem in communication is the illusion that it has taken place."

– George Bernard Shaw

It's Easy to Slip

Life gets busy. Writing emails feels like work. You don't want to annoy people. Or maybe you're just not sure what to say.

So you delay. You skip a week. Then another. Before long, it feels awkward to send *anything*, so you don't. Been there. But here's what we've learned:

Consistency builds trust. Silence builds distance.

Emailing Doesn't Mean Selling Every Time

Let's clear something up: Emailing regularly doesn't mean pitching every day. It means showing up. Adding value. Staying top of mind.

Sometimes it's:

- A tip
- A story
- A case study
- A behind-the-scenes peek
- A friendly nudge
- Or yes... a great offer

You're building a relationship, not just blasting promotions.

We've Watched Lists Die and Lists Thrive

One of Frank's clients had a 10,000-person email list... and hadn't emailed in 6 months. They sent a re-engagement sequence and over 3,000 people unsubscribed immediately. Not because the content was bad, but because they forgot who he was.

Compare that to another client who emailed weekly with tips and updates. When it came time to launch a product? Her list was ready. Engaged. Warm. And the sales flowed.

Bret had a colleague who had built up a list of 55,000+ people in the financial services sector. Not too shabby.

He hired a "guru" to help him craft an email to be sent to his list. Problem was the "tone" of that email was a polar opposite to what they had come to expect from this person. It was not "on brand" with what they'd come to expect from this person.

So it began to happen almost immediately once they hit the send button. Unsubscribe - unsubscribe - unsubscribe. When all was said and done a list that had once been over 55,000 people was a list of just 5,000 people. Ouch.

Your Action Step

Open your email platform and ask yourself:

- When was the last time I sent something?
- If I emailed tomorrow, would they remember me?
- What kind of content could I send *just to be helpful*?

Now… schedule one email this week. Even a short tip or a quick story. Just reconnect. Then do it again next week. And the next.

Bottom line?

Your list isn't a trophy, it's a conversation. So stop ghosting your subscribers. Start showing up like someone worth listening to.

Chapter 42: Using Boring Subject Lines That Never Get Opened

You know the feeling. You've spent 45 minutes crafting the perfect email. It's helpful. It's clear. It's got a great offer.

You hit send, sit back, and wait. And then... Nothing.

Barely any opens. No clicks. Just radio silence from a list you *know* asked to hear from you. So what happened?

You lost the battle in the subject line.

Yep. The one-liner that decides if your email gets opened... or trashed without a second thought.

The 5-Second Test

Every day, your subscriber opens their inbox to a mini war zone. Dozens, sometimes hundreds, of messages fighting for attention.

So unless your subject line stands out, sparks curiosity, or promises something that matters... it's going to get skipped. Your subject line isn't just a label. It's your **ticket in.**

Why Most Subject Lines Fail

Here's what we see too often:

- "Just a quick update"
- "October Newsletter"
- "Tips for your business"

Look, we get it. You don't want to sound salesy. You don't want to overpromise. But if you lead with something generic, safe, or vague, you're done. The trash icon wins.

Because bland subject lines don't get opened. And unopened emails don't make sales.

People Don't Click on Boring

A quick story - Frank once helped a client whose email open rates had completely tanked. Her content? Great. Her timing? Spot on.

But her subject lines? They read like chapter titles from a textbook.

They swapped out those headlines for real, punchy subject lines, stuff like:

- "Can I be brutally honest?"
- "This nearly ruined my launch"

- "Read this before Friday…"

Suddenly, people started opening. Reading. Clicking.

Her words didn't change. The *doorway* did.

It's Not About Tricks, It's About Interest

A good subject line doesn't trick someone into opening.
It **tells them there's something inside worth seeing.**

That could be a story. A solution. A confession. A surprise.
But it needs to *feel like something they can't scroll past.*

Not because it's hyped up. Because it's human. Real. Relevant.

Your Action Step

Next time you write an email, don't just slap on a label. Stop and ask yourself "Would I open this?"

If not, try again. Push a little harder. Loosen the tie. Don't write what sounds safe, write what sounds **interesting**.

Then send it. Track it. And build your own vault of subject lines that get the job done.

Bottom line?

It doesn't matter how great your message is if no one opens it. So, make your subject lines impossible to ignore.

Not loud. Not clickbait. Just *too good to scroll past.*

Chapter 43: Writing Emails That Sound Corporate, Not Personal

Let's be real. Nobody ever said, "Wow, I can't wait to open this email from a faceless brand using a formal tone and buzzwords!"

Yet every day, inboxes are filled with emails that read like they were written by a robot in a cubicle trying way too hard to sound important.

> **"Dear Valued Subscriber,**
> **We wanted to take this opportunity to inform you..."**

Yikes. If your emails sound like they were drafted by a lawyer in a three-piece suit, you're doing it wrong.

People don't want polished perfection. They want personality. They want *you*.

Email Isn't a Press Release, It's a Conversation

We don't care if you're emailing one person or 10,000... it should feel like it came from **one person to one person.**

Like you just slid into their inbox to share something helpful, encouraging, or insightful. Because at the end of the day, that's what email is, it's **personal.**

Not corporate. Not stiff. Not cold. So, stop writing like a boardroom memo and start writing like someone they'd really want to hear from.

Talk Like You Talk

You don't need to "elevate your language" to sound professional. You need to sound **Authentic. Relatable. Human.**

That means contractions. That means "hey," "just checking in," and "you're gonna love this." That means ditching the jargon and writing like you'd speak over coffee.

We've seen emails with typos outperform emails that were proofread to perfection. Why? Because people connected with the voice. It felt real.

There was a time we thought being taken seriously meant writing like we were submitting a term paper. The emails were long-winded. Over-explained. Way too formal.

Guess what? The engagement was awful. Nobody replied. Fewer people clicked. The list felt dead.

So, we stripped it all down. Started writing like we were talking to a friend. Like we're talking to *you* right now.

And boom, everything changed. People started replying. Thanking us. Buying. Not because the content changed, but because the **tone** did.

Your Action Step

Look at your last email.

Does it sound like something you'd say out loud? If not, rewrite it until it does. If it reads like it came from "Company Communications," kill it.

You want your reader to nod their head as they read. To feel like *you're in their corner.* Because that's what builds trust.

Bottom line?

Your subscribers don't want another formal, polished brand message. They want *you.* Your voice. Your insight. Your honesty.

So write like a real person. And watch your emails actually start working.

Chapter 44: No Onboarding Sequence for New Subscribers

Here's the scenario:

Someone joins your list. Maybe they grabbed your lead magnet, signed up for a webinar, or opted in for your newsletter.

They're interested. They're warm. They're ready to hear more. And then... crickets.

No welcome. No intro. No value. No direction.

Just silence, until maybe, weeks later, they get tossed into a generic email blast they weren't expecting and barely remember signing up for. You just lost them.

No onboarding = no relationship.

And in the online world, if people don't connect early, they disconnect fast.

First Impressions Stick

Your onboarding sequence is like the welcome mat to your business. It sets the tone. It tells your story. It shows them what to expect and why they should care.

Without it, people feel lost. Or worse, forgotten.

Think of it like inviting someone into your store... and then walking away without saying a word. That's what skipping onboarding feels like.

But I'm Not Sure What to Send...

This is where a lot of people freeze.

They think onboarding has to be some 12-email, perfectly automated sequence with storytelling arcs, trigger links, and behavioral segments.

Nah. Keep it simple. What does someone **need to know** once they join your world?

- Who are you?

- What do you help with?

- What should they expect from your emails?

- How can they get more value or take the next step?

If you can answer those questions in 3–5 short emails, you're already ahead of most.

The Missed Opportunity

We can't tell you how many times we've seen someone go through the trouble of creating a great lead magnet... only to let that new subscriber drift off into the void.

No follow-up. No introduction. Nothing. That's like putting gas in the car and never turning the key. If someone joins your list, that's momentum. Use it. This is your chance to:

- Build trust.

- Showcase your best content.

- Set expectations.

- Lead them to the next logical step (buy, book, engage).

Your Action Step

If you don't have a welcome or onboarding sequence in place, start with this:

1. Write a simple **"Welcome to my world"** email. Introduce yourself. Thank them. Tell them what to expect.

2. Follow up with an email that points to your **most valuable free resource** (blog post, video, etc.).

3. Add a third email that shares **your origin story** or a client win, something that builds connection and credibility.

4. Close the loop with a fourth email that includes a **clear next step**, book a call, grab your offer, and join your group.

Once that's in place, you can always expand later.

Bottom line?

If you don't guide your new subscribers, someone else will.

Don't let your list go cold before it even gets warm. Say hello. Build the bridge. And turn new leads into lifelong customers.

Chapter 45: Ignoring Segmentation (Sending the Same Thing to Everyone)

Let's imagine this for a second…

You walk into a room full of people. Some are total beginners. Some are advanced pros. A few are past customers. Some just heard about you for the first time yesterday.

And you stand up, clear your throat, and say:

> "Hey everyone, I've got one thing to say,
> and it applies to all of you the same way, no
> matter where you're at."

Think that's gonna land? Of course not.

But that's exactly what most people are doing when they send **one blanket email** to their entire list, regardless of who's on it, where they're at, or what they need.

When you treat everyone the same, you connect with no one.

Not All Subscribers Are Created Equal

One of the biggest email marketing mistakes we see is this "blast everyone" approach.

- New subscribers get the same message as people who've been on your list for years.

- People who already bought your product get pitched... the same product.

- Someone who's just learning the ropes gets hit with advanced tips they don't understand.

- Someone who's ready to buy gets more beginner-level freebies instead of a clear next step.

It's like trying to feed steak to a toddler and formula to a bodybuilder. You *might* get lucky... but odds are, you're going to confuse a lot of people, and lose their attention in the process.

Why Segmentation Matters

Here's the thing:

Your list isn't just a bunch of names. It's a group of people, each with their own story, needs, and stage of the journey.

When you segment, you speak to *where someone is right now*. And that's what makes them feel seen, understood, and more likely to engage.

Segmentation isn't just about organizing your list. It's about **connecting better.**

You send the right message to the right person at the right time, and that makes all the difference.

We Didn't Segment at First Either

We'll be honest, we didn't start out segmenting. At first, we just blasted everyone with the same updates. Easier, right?

But then we realized something weird. Some people were unsubscribing after they received a product promo. Others were disengaging when they were sent basic tips.

Turns out, we were sending offers to people who had already bought… and sending beginner-level tips to folks who were way past that.

It wasn't that the content was bad, it was that it wasn't **relevant** to them anymore.

Once we started tagging people, buyers, non-buyers, course students, freebie seekers, we could tailor what we sent. Open rates went up. Sales increased. Replies came in.

Not because we sent *more* emails. But because we sent **better-targeted ones.**

Start Simple

Segmentation doesn't have to be complicated. You don't need 38 tags and a PhD in automation.

Just ask yourself:

- Has this person bought from me before?
- What lead magnet did they opt-in through?
- Are they more beginner or advanced?
- What topic are they most interested in?

Even dividing your list into just two or three core groups is a game-changer. And most email tools make this easy with tags or segments. (If yours doesn't, it might be time for a new tool.)

Your Action Step

Take a look at your list today and ask:

- Who are my **buyers**?
- Who are my **brand-new leads**?
- Who's **clicked** but never purchased?

Tag 'em.

Then start crafting your next email **with one segment in mind.** Talk directly to that person like you know where they're at and what they need.

That's how you build trust. That's how you boost engagement. And that's how you make people feel like you honestly get them. Because you do.

Bottom line?

The more personal your message feels the more powerful it becomes. Don't shout into the crowd. Speak to the person in the room who's already leaning in.

Chapter 46: Failing to Deliver Value Before Pitching

Let's put it this way:

> If the first thing your subscriber hears from you is a sales pitch... don't be surprised when it's also the *last* thing they hear.

Imagine meeting someone at a networking event, and before you can even shake their hand, they shove a brochure in your face and say, "Hey, wanna buy my thing?"

Awkward, right? Now, think about your email list. You worked hard to get people to sign up, offering a lead magnet, a freebie, and a promise of help.

They trusted you with their email address. And your first response? A pitch? Yeah... not great.

It's Not That Pitching Is Bad

Let's clear this up, **you should absolutely make offers.** That's how businesses survive. You have something valuable to sell, and people need to hear about it.

But the problem comes when you skip the relationship-building part and go straight for the wallet.

Trust comes first. Value comes first. Then comes the offer.

When you lead with helpful insights, actionable tips, or even just a friendly "here's how I can help you" email, people start to feel like you're on their side, not just in it for the sale.

People Don't Buy from Strangers, They Buy from Guides

A good friend and marketing mentor of ours, Armand Morin would say "You haven't earned the right to ask for the sale yet!".

You don't have to wait forever to pitch. You just need to *show up with value first.*

- Maybe that's a helpful tip
- Maybe it's a quick story with a takeaway
- Maybe it's a video, a cheat sheet, or a blog post that makes their life a little easier

When people feel like they've already gained something from you *before* they've spent a dime, the pitch doesn't feel like a money grab. It feels like the *next logical step.*

We've Made This Mistake (And Paid for It)

Early on, we were so excited to share an offer that we'd fire off a sales email the moment someone joined a list.

We figured, "They opted in, they're ready!"

But all that came back was silence… and unsubscribes.

When we slowed down and sent a few emails delivering value first, sharing tools, telling stories, and giving actionable advice, something shifted.

People started replying. They were more engaged. They clicked more. Bought more.

Why? Because there was trust. And trust comes from *giving*, not just asking.

Your Action Step

Before you send your next promotional email, ask yourself:

- Have I earned their attention?
- Have I offered something useful first?
- Does this feel like a conversation… or a transaction?

If the answer feels a little off, go back and deliver value. Even one helpful email, tip, or insight can reset the tone and reconnect the relationship.

Bottom line?

Selling is part of business, but **leading with value is what makes people want to buy.**

Give first. Pitch second. You won't just make more sales, you'll build a list of people who *actually look forward to hearing from you.*

Chapter 47: Not Testing and Tracking Email Performance

Here's a simple question…

> If your email didn't get opened, didn't get clicked, and didn't lead to a sale, would you even know?

For a lot of business owners, the honest answer is… *no.*

They hit "send," cross their fingers, and hope something happens. But hope isn't a strategy. And it definitely isn't data.

> **If you're not tracking what's working (and what's not), you're flying blind.**

When you don't track, you can't improve. When you can't improve, you stay stuck in the same cycle: Low open rates. Weak clicks. Disappointing results.

Data Isn't Scary, It's a Shortcut

We get it. The word "analytics" makes some folks break into a cold sweat. But testing your emails isn't about turning into a numbers nerd. It's about **getting clarity** on what actually moves the needle.

It's the difference between:

- Guessing what subject lines work... vs. *knowing*.
- Hoping people click... vs. *seeing* where they stop.
- Blasting emails... vs. *optimizing* them.

It's not about having perfect stats. It's about paying attention.

The Basics You Should Be Watching

Let's keep it simple. If you just tracked these three things, you'd be ahead of 90% of online business owners:

1. **Open rate** – Are people opening your emails?
2. **Click-through rate** – Are they engaging with your links?
3. **Unsubscribes** – Are you losing people with the wrong message?

If your open rate tanks, maybe your subject line needs work. If clicks are low, maybe your call-to-action isn't clear. If unsubscribes spike, maybe you're sending the wrong content to the wrong segment.

See? These numbers tell a story. Once you understand that story, you can start rewriting it in your favor.

Ignoring the Numbers Can Cost You Big

We used to send emails and move on. Didn't really look at the results. Thought, *"Well, that one felt good."* But one day we checked in and realized we'd been getting lower and lower opens for weeks.

Why? We had started using new subject lines that sounded more "professional" … and less like us.

The solution? We went back to more personal, curiosity-driven lines. Open rates bounced right back up. That's the power of testing.

Your Action Step

This week, pull up your last 3 email campaigns.

Look at:

- What got opened?
- What got clicked?
- What got ignored?

Now ask:

- What can I tweak next time?
- Can I A/B test two subject lines?
- Should I resend to un-opens with a new angle?

Don't overthink it, just start paying attention. Because small tweaks, based on real data, lead to big improvements over time.

Bottom line?

If you're not testing, you're guessing. And if you're not tracking, you're missing out on what could be working even better.

Check the numbers. Test what matters. And start sending smarter, not just more.

Chapter 48: Forgetting to Link to Your Offer or Site in the Email

You might laugh when you read this one. It sounds like such a rookie mistake.

But we promise you, we've seen seasoned marketers, coaches, and even copywriters... hit send on a beautiful, persuasive email and completely forget the one thing that actually gets people to take action: **The link.**

Yep. No link to the product. No link to the landing page. No link to the calendar, the course, the download, nothing. And just like that, all the effort... wasted.

Don't Make Them Work for It

Here's something you need to understand about your readers:

They're not going to hunt for your offer.

They won't Google your website. They won't reply asking how to buy. They won't magically find your sales page on their own.

If you don't tell them where to go, and make it **dead simple to get there**, they're gone.

Not because they didn't want to take action. But because you didn't make it easy enough. A quick rule of thumb is to include three links when possible in your email.

We've Done It Too (And Felt the Pain)

We'll admit it... We've sent more than one email where we got all wrapped up in the story, the teaching, the setup, and completely forgot to include the actual link.

No button. No text link. Nothing.

We remember one campaign that had an incredible engagement. People replying. Saying how much they enjoyed the email. But no sales.

Why? Because we never gave them the *path* to the offer. Talk about a facepalm moment.

You Can't Assume They Know What to Do

Sometimes people will write an email, mention their product, and think, *"Well, they know where to find it."*

But here's the deal:

> If you don't spell it out clearly and
> confidently, most people won't act.

They need direction. Not "check out my site sometime..."

But:

"Click here to grab your copy now."
"Reserve your spot before registration closes."
"Download the guide instantly here."

Make the action clear. Make the link obvious. And don't be shy about including it more than once.

Your Action Step

Before you send your next email, pause and check:

- Did I include a clear call to action?
- Did I link directly to what I'm talking about?
- Is the link visible, not buried, not hidden?

If not, fix it. Because even the best email won't convert if you don't give people a **bridge** to walk over.

Bottom line?

If you don't include the link, you've killed your conversion before it even had a chance. So don't be subtle. Don't make 'em guess.

Tell them where to go. Give them the link. And watch your emails actually do what they're supposed to do.

Chapter 49: Letting Your Email List Go Cold

Building an email list is hard work.

You create the lead magnet. Set up the opt-in. You start collecting names. Each subscriber is someone who said, *"Yeah, I'm interested in what you've got."*

And then what do a lot of business owners do? Absolutely nothing. No welcome. No value. They let weeks, or even months, go by without sending a single email.

Then, when it's finally time to launch something or make an offer, they suddenly show up in the inbox like, *"Hey, remember me?"*

Spoiler alert: They don't.

Out of Sight = Out of Trust

Here's what you need to understand about your list: **It's a relationship.** And like any relationship, it needs attention to stay alive.

When people don't hear from you for a long period, they forget why they signed up in the first place.

Worse, when you finally do send an email, they're either confused, disengaged… or they unsubscribe. Not because they don't care. But because *you stopped showing up*.

We Get It, Life Happens

You get busy. You miss a week. Then another. Suddenly it feels awkward to send anything at all.

You think, *"Well now it's been so long… I'm not even sure what to say."* That's normal.

But here's the truth:

The longer you wait, the harder it gets.

And the colder your list becomes, the less likely it is to warm back up.

A Cold List Is a Costly One

Letting your email list go cold doesn't just hurt your open rates, it hurts your business.

- You lose out on engagement
- You lose out on feedback
- You lose out on *sales*

And if you've got a large list you're paying for every month? That's money going out... with nothing coming back in.

You're sitting on potential, and letting it drift away.

Rewarming Is Possible (But It's Work)

Now, the good news? You *can* bring a cold list back to life. But you have to earn back attention. You have to reintroduce yourself. You have to deliver consistent value before you ask for anything.

It's not a one-and-done email. It's a campaign. A story. A few "Hey, I know it's been a while" messages that give value, rebuild trust, and get people excited again.

Your Action Step

Be honest: has your list gone cold?

If so, start re-engaging this week:

1. Send a personal, honest email: "Hey, it's been a minute..."
2. Share a quick tip, a story, or something useful, **no pitch yet.**
3. Ask a question or give them something to click on (engagement wakes up your deliverability).
4. Keep showing up consistently from here on out, even if it's just once a week.

Because the only way to build a warm, responsive list... is to stop ghosting it.

Bottom line?

If you don't talk to your list, someone else will. And that relationship you worked so hard to start?

It'll fade. So show up. Even if it's been a while. Especially if it's been a while. Your list is only as valuable as the connection you keep alive.

Chapter 50: No Easy Unsubscribe or Compliance with Email Laws (like CAN-SPAM)

We know this isn't the flashiest topic in the world, but hear us out...

> If you're not making it easy for people to unsubscribe, or worse, ignoring email compliance laws, you're not just being annoying... You could be risking your entire business.

Look, we get it. You worked hard to build your email list. Every subscriber feels like a tiny win. So the idea of letting someone leave? That can sting a little.

But trust us, **the worst thing you can do is try to force them to stay.**

Don't Hold Your List Hostage

We've all been there:

You scroll to the bottom of an email to unsubscribe and...
There's no link. Or worse, it takes you to a login page. Or makes you fill out a form. Or says it'll take "10 business days" to process.

That's not clever. That's shady. And shady doesn't build trust. It gets you flagged. Reported. Blacklisted.

> If someone doesn't want to hear from you anymore, let them go with dignity.

Because the truth is, it's better to have a smaller, *engaged* list than a bloated one full of people who are mentally checked out, or worse, marking you as spam.

You Have Legal Responsibilities

This isn't just about being courteous, it's about **staying compliant.**

Laws like **CAN-SPAM (in the U.S.)** and **GDPR (in Europe)** are very clear:

- You must provide a clear and visible way to unsubscribe.
- You must include your physical mailing address.
- You must not use deceptive subject lines or sender names.
- And you *must* honor unsubscribes promptly.

Violating these laws can result in serious penalties. We're talking **thousands of dollars per email** in fines if someone decides to report you.

And guess what? Email service providers are watching too.

If you rack up too many spam complaints or hard
bounces, your deliverability tanks, even for the people
who *do* want to hear from you.

Respect = Retention

Here's something most people forget:

> Giving people the freedom to leave makes
> them *more likely* to stay.

When someone knows they can opt-out anytime, no
games, no hoops, they're more comfortable opting *in*. It
builds trust. And trust keeps lists healthy.

Your Action Step

Check your last few email campaigns.

- Is your unsubscribe link easy to find?
- Does it work properly?
- Are you including your physical business
  address?
- Do your emails follow your country's compliance
  laws?

If any of those are missing, fix it now.

And while you're at it, take a look at your email
platform's default settings. Most of them make this
easy, you just need to make sure it's set up right.

Bottom line?

Trying to trap people on your list isn't clever, it's a liability. Make it easy to leave. Stay compliant. And build your list on respect, not restriction.

Because when you treat people right, the right people stick around.

Customer Experience Mistakes

You got the sale, awesome. But what happens next?

Because here's the truth:

The transaction isn't the finish line. It's the starting point.

A lot of online business owners work so hard to *get* the customer, that they forget what really matters, **keeping** them.

And that comes down to experience.

- Are you delivering what was promised?
- Are your customers feeling taken care of, or totally forgotten the moment they click "buy"?
- Are you making it easy to love doing business with you?

This section dives into the often-overlooked details that shape your customer's journey, and influence whether they come back, refer others, or quietly disappear.

Because in the end, people don't just remember the product. They remember how you made them feel.

Let's make sure they remember you for the right reasons.

Chapter 51: Hard-to-Navigate Checkouts or a Confusing Buying Process

Let's say someone loves what you offer. They're ready to buy. They click the button…

And then? They hit a wall.

- A slow-loading cart.
- A form with 18 unnecessary fields.
- A checkout page that looks sketchy or asks them to create an account *before* they pay.
- Or worse, there's no clear path at all, and they have to click around like they're solving a maze.

So what do they do? They bail. And just like that, a hot prospect turns cold, because you made buying harder than it needed to be.

"A Confused Buyer Never Buys."
- Donald Miller

You're Losing Sales You Never Knew You Had

This is the worst kind of business leak.

People are clicking "Buy Now," which means you've done 90% of the work. They're in the mindset. They've made the decision.

But if your checkout process is clunky, confusing, or overly complicated, you're giving them time to second-guess. In the world of online business, **friction kills momentum.**

Simple = Profitable

Your checkout should be dead simple. Click. See the offer. Fill out the form. Pay. Done. That's it.

No unnecessary distractions. No confusing upsell trees that feel like traps. No surprise fees at the end.

We've reviewed so many sites where the checkout feels like it was built by someone who *never actually tested it as a customer.*

Here's what we always say:

> If it takes longer to buy from you than it takes to lose interest... you're losing sales.

A Personal Story (with a Real Price Tag)

Frank once had a client who was frustrated about low sales. The funnel was solid. The offer was great. But after doing a test purchase, he found the "Buy Now" button took you to a generic cart, **with no product pre-selected.**

You had to *go find the product again* on the order page.

How many people do you think figured that out? Almost none.

A two-minute fix led to a 42% increase in completed purchases. Not because we changed the offer, because we removed the friction.

Your Action Step

Go test your own checkout, on desktop and mobile.

- Does the button work?
- Is the process clear?
- Can you go from "click" to "complete" in under a minute?
- Are there distractions, hidden costs, or steps that don't need to be there?

Better yet, have someone else try it. Watch what they struggle with. Then simplify, streamline, and smooth it out.

Bottom line?

Don't let a messy checkout process kill your momentum.
Make it easy. Make it trustworthy. Make it so simple,
they can buy before doubt creeps in.

Because if they're ready to hand you their money...
Don't make them work for it.

Chapter 52: No Clear Contact or Support Option

Here's the deal:

> If people don't know how to reach you, they start wondering if they even *should*.

You can have the best offer in the world, the slickest funnel, the most beautifully designed site… but if there's no clear way for someone to get help, ask a question, or feel like there's a real person behind the screen?

You're losing trust. Fast. And in the world of online business, **trust is everything.**

"Is Anyone Even There?"

We've all been on sites where he had a legitimate question before we were ready to buy. Simple stuff, too. Like:

- "How long will this take to ship?"
- "Can I use this if I'm outside the U.S.?"
- "Does this work with [specific software]?"

But guess what? No phone number. No email. No chat. No form. Just a sad little FAQ section that *almost* answered the question, but not quite.

And you know what we do? We leave.

Because if we're already getting frustrated before we give you money, we're not sticking around to see what happens *after*.

Silence Is a Dealbreaker

People want to know that if something goes wrong, someone has their back. If you hide your contact info or bury your support options like it's a treasure hunt, it sends the wrong message.

It says, "We don't want to hear from you." Even if that's not your intention, that's how it feels to the customer.

And if your offer feels risky, unfamiliar, or too good to be true? The lack of support info just confirms their doubts.

You Don't Have to Offer 24/7 Live Chat

Now, let's be clear, We're not saying you need a full-blown customer service team answering calls around the clock.

But you *do* need something. Something simple. Something obvious.

- A visible contact page
- An email address that works

- A support form that gets a real response
- Even an FAQ page *with* a backup option if their question isn't covered

The key? Make it easy. Make it obvious. Make it human.

Your Action Step

Visit your website like you're a first-time customer.

- Can you find a "Contact" or "Support" link in 3 seconds or less?
- Does it lead to a helpful, real option, or a dead end?
- Would *you* feel confident buying from this site if you needed help?

If the answer is no, fix it. It doesn't take much, and it makes a massive difference in conversions, and in customer satisfaction down the road.

Bottom line?

People buy from businesses they trust. And one of the fastest ways to build, or break, that trust is how easy it is to get in touch.

So don't make them guess. Show them you're real. Show them you care. And you'll be the one they remember when it's time to buy.

Chapter 53: Not Responding Quickly to Customer Inquiries

So here's a question:

> When someone reaches out to you with a
> question, how long do they wait before they
> hear back?

If it's more than a day… you've got a problem. In fact, **if it's more than a few hours**, you might already be losing them.

In the online world, response time equals perceived value. People want answers now. Not next week. Not "when you get around to it."

They've got options. If you're not there when they reach out, they'll find someone who is.

You Don't Have to Be Fast… You Have to Be *Present*

Now, I'm not saying you need to be glued to your inbox 24/7. That's not realistic, and it's not healthy.

But you *do* need to have a system.

When people send in questions or concerns, whether it's pre-sale or post-sale, they're looking for **reassurance.**

They want to know:

- "Can I trust this person?"
- "Will I be taken care of?"
- "Did my order actually go through?"
- "Is there a human on the other end of this?"

If you're slow to respond, or worse, you don't respond at all, you've just added friction to a relationship that was already a little fragile.

The Moment They're Waiting… They're Doubting

We've had situations where we bought something and emailed with a quick question… then didn't hear back for three days.

By the time we got a reply, a refund had already been requested. Not because the product was bad, but because the silence made us uneasy.

And that's what silence does, it breeds uncertainty. If someone's on the fence about buying and you take too long to answer their question?

Fence-sitters fall off. And they don't usually land in your favor.

You Don't Have to Do It All Yourself

The good news is: this doesn't have to be you replying to every single email personally.

You can:

- Set up an auto-reply that says, "Hey, we got your message, here's when you can expect a reply."

- Use a help desk tool or shared inbox so someone on your team can handle inquiries.

- Create a simple internal FAQ for your team (or yourself) to copy/paste clear answers.

- At a minimum, check your inbox at key points during the day so you're not leaving people hanging.

People don't expect instant answers. But they do expect **acknowledgment.** And that's what makes the difference.

Your Action Step

Run a quick test: send yourself a question through your own contact form or support email.

- How fast do you respond?
- What does the confirmation message say (if anything)?
- Would you feel taken care of if you were on the other end?

If the experience feels cold, confusing, or delayed, fix it. Even a little automation or clarity goes a long way.

Bottom line?

Responsiveness isn't just good customer service, it's smart business. Be the business that replies. Be the business that follows up. Be the business that people *talk about* for all the right reasons.

Because in a world full of silence, your quick response might be the loudest trust signal of all.

Chapter 54: Over-Promising and Under-Delivering

Let's call it what it is:

> Nothing will tank your credibility faster
> than making a big promise... and then not
> delivering on it.

We've all seen the hype:

"Explode your traffic overnight!"
"Make $10K in 24 hours with no experience!"
"Lose 30 pounds by Friday!"

Sure, it might get clicks. Might even get a few sales. But what if what you deliver doesn't live up to the expectation?

You've just lost trust, and maybe that customer for good.

Short-Term Sales vs. Long-Term Reputation

Here's what we've learned over the years:

> It's better to surprise people with how much
> they *get*... then disappoint them with how
> much they *don't*.

You can push hard on urgency, scarcity, even bold claims, **as long as you can back it up.**

But once people start feeling like they were tricked, misled, or oversold... they won't just refund.

- They'll tell their friends
- They'll leave reviews
- They'll quietly unsubscribe and never look back

And that's way more expensive than just losing a sale.

It's Not Just What You Say, It's What You Imply

Sometimes over-promising doesn't even come from the actual copy, it comes from **how it's positioned.**

You show a screenshot of one big result but don't clarify it's not typical. You hint that something's easier or faster than it really is. You imply "instant" when the truth is... it takes time, effort, or learning.

People buy based on expectations. And if you set the wrong one, even unintentionally, you've already started the customer experience with disappointment.

There was a product FrankI launched early on that he was proud of. He knew it could help people. But in his excitement, he made the mistake of overselling the outcome.

He didn't lie, but he didn't fully clarify the time and work involved either. It sold well... at first.

But then came the refund requests. The "this isn't what I thought it was" emails. The hard truth is that he'd sold the result, but didn't set up the journey right.

Lesson learned.

We strongly recommend that you *under-promise and over-deliver* because that creates happy surprises, not customer complaints.

Your Action Step

Take a look at your current offer, funnel, or email sequence.

- Are you making promises you can consistently keep?
- Are you setting the right expectations from the first touchpoint?
- Could a first-time buyer be disappointed if they take your copy at face value?

If the answer is "maybe," clean it up. Be clear. Be confident. But be **real.**

Bottom line?

Big promises might get you sales. But consistent

delivery is what gets you *loyal customers.* Say what you'll do. Then do it. Or better, do *more* than they expected.

Because your reputation is the one thing your competitors can't copy.

Chapter 55: No Onboarding or Welcome Experience Post-Sale

You did it.

The sale came through. The confirmation hit your inbox. Your customer clicked *Buy Now* and put their trust (and money) in you.

Now what? If the answer is… nothing. That's a big problem.

> **The moment after the sale is when the real relationship begins.**

And yet, most online businesses completely drop the ball here.

- No thank-you
- No welcome message
- No instructions
- No next steps

Just silence. And in that silence, your customer is left wondering: "Did I just make a mistake?"

Confirmation ≠ Connection

Sure, maybe your shopping cart sent out a receipt. But that's not a welcome experience, that's just a transaction summary.

What people want after they buy is reassurance. A sense that they're in the right place. They want to know what to do next, where to go, and what to expect.

When they don't get that? Doubt creeps in. Support tickets go up. Refund requests follow.

And all because you didn't take 10 minutes to say, "Hey, welcome aboard, let's get you started."

Your Customer Is Still Listening

Right after the sale, your customer is at their highest level of attention. They're excited. They're curious. They're ready to engage. So don't waste that window by going quiet.

Use it to:

- Reaffirm their decision
- Set clear expectations
- Help them get their first *win*
- Point them toward helpful content or next steps
- Show them you actually give a rip about their experience

We've Seen This Save Sales

Frank once worked with a client whose refund rate was creeping higher than they liked.

The product was solid. The checkout worked fine. But when Frank signed up to mystery shop the process, he noticed something strange…

After he paid, he got **no real onboarding**. No welcome. No helpful next steps. Just a plain download link and a bland receipt.

They added a simple 3-email post-sale sequence, one welcome, one "how to get started," and one short tip with a bonus.

- Refunds dropped 37%
- Engagement spiked
- People stayed because they felt taken care of

That's the power of onboarding.

Your Action Step

If you don't already have one, it's time to create a basic welcome experience:

1. **Thank them.** Let them know you appreciate their trust.

2. **Guide them.** Show them how to access what they bought or use it properly.
3. **Support them.** Let them know how to get help if they get stuck.
4. **Encourage them.** Point out the next logical win they should aim for.
5. **Invite them.** Share how they can stay connected, through your community, newsletter, or next offer.

You don't have to overcomplicate it. Just be present. Be helpful. Be human.

Bottom line?

People don't want to feel like just another order number.
They want to feel seen. Supported. Guided.

So give them more than a receipt. Give them an experience that sets the tone for everything to come.

Chapter 56: Making Customers Feel Like Transactions, Not Relationships

Let's be honest… No one wants to feel like a number. They want to feel like they matter.

And yet, so many online businesses treat their customers like they're just another notch in the sales column.

You can see it a mile away:

- The cold, generic emails after purchase

- The zero follow-up after delivery

- The lack of acknowledgment, appreciation, or even a simple "Hey, how's it going?"

The message it sends?

"Thanks for your money. Good luck."

And that's how you turn a first-time buyer into a one-time buyer.

People Don't Remember the Transaction, They Remember How You Made Them Feel

This might sound soft, but it's true. Your product might be great. Your funnel might be slick. But if the customer walks away feeling like they were just part of a sales process then... you've lost the emotional connection.

And that's what drives loyalty, referrals, and long-term success.

The best businesses don't just deliver, they **connect**. They make their customers feel seen, heard, and appreciated.

We've Been on Both Sides

Frank remembers buying a program once where the pre-sale experience was fantastic. Daily emails. Videos. Bonuses. All the bells and whistles.

But after he hit "Buy"? Crickets.

No thank-you. No check-in. No "How can we help?" It was like he'd served his purpose, and now he was on my own.

Contrast that with another company that followed up a week after he bought, just to say, "Hey, how's it going? Need help with anything?"

Which one do you think he bought from again? Exactly.

It Doesn't Take Much

Here's the good news: building real relationships doesn't require fancy automation or a huge team.

It just takes intention.

- A short check-in email post-purchase.
- A handwritten thank-you note if you're shipping physical products.
- A follow-up question like "What's your biggest challenge right now?"
- A personal reply when someone reaches out, instead of a cold autoresponder.

These little touches make a big difference. Because when people feel cared for, they stick around. And they tell others.

Your Action Step

Take a look at your customer journey:

- Where are you making people feel like a person?
- And where are you treating them like a transaction?

Be honest. Then find one spot to inject a little humanity.

One small moment to say, "I see you. I appreciate you. I've got your back."

It doesn't have to be big. It just has to be *real*.

Bottom line?

Customers remember how you made them feel long after they forgot what they paid for.

So, treat every sale like the start of a relationship, not the end of a transaction.

Be human. Be helpful. And you won't just win a customer, you'll earn a fan.

Chapter 57: Lack of Personalization in Support or Follow-Up

Let's talk about something that's easy to overlook, but impossible to ignore once you've felt it.

> **That moment when you realize you're just ticket #872.**

You reach out with a question, maybe even a problem. And what comes back?

A generic, copy-paste reply that doesn't address what you said… doesn't acknowledge *you*… and honestly feels like it could've gone to anybody.

It stings a little, right?

Because when people take the time to reach out, they're not just looking for an answer. They're looking for a *connection*.

Robotic Doesn't Build Relationships

Look, templates and canned replies aren't the enemy. They save time. They create consistency. But when they're not used carefully?

They feel cold. Impersonal. Lazy.

If your response sounds like a corporate chatbot spit it out, especially in a small business setting, you're missing the whole point of customer support.

Support isn't just about solving problems.
It's about making people feel heard.

A Tiny Touch of Humanity Goes a Long Way

Here's what we've found:

You don't have to write a novel. You don't have to memorize every customer's name and backstory.

But you *do* need to personalize your communication just enough to say, "Hey, I see you."

That might be:

- Using their first name
- Mentioning the specific issue they reached out about
- Referencing something they bought
- Closing your email with a human tone, not "Regards, Customer Success Team"

This stuff isn't fluff, it's *fuel* for loyalty.

We Had to Learn This Ourselves

Back when we both started responding to support emails personally, we'd sometimes rush through them, get the answer out, move on.

But when we slowed down... added a first name... even just said, "Hey, thanks again for grabbing the product..." the tone changed.

People wrote back. They appreciated the help. They stuck around. And they remembered *us,* not just the brand.

That's what creates customers for life.

Your Action Step

Next time you reply to a customer, or set up an autoresponder, ask yourself:

- Does this feel like it came from a real person?
- Have I acknowledged who they are and what they asked?
- Would *I* feel good getting this message?

If the answer's no... tweak it. Even one extra sentence of personalization can change everything.

Bottom line?

People don't want perfect. They want *personal.* So, ditch the script when it counts. Take a breath. Be real. Be present. Because a little personalization can turn a routine support ticket into a relationship-building moment.

Chapter 58: Failing to Gather Feedback and Reviews

Here's a quick question for you:

> After someone buys from you... do you ever ask them what they thought?

Because if you're not gathering feedback or asking for reviews, you're leaving a mountain of value on the table.

We're talking about insight. Social proof. Trust builders. Conversion boosters. All just sitting there untapped because nobody asked.

It's one of the easiest ways to improve your business... and one of the most overlooked.

Silence Doesn't Mean Satisfaction

Just because someone didn't complain doesn't mean they loved the experience. And just because someone was *happy* doesn't mean they'll *automatically* leave a glowing review.

You have to ask. Period.

If you wait around hoping people will offer feedback on their own, you'll usually just hear from the outliers, either the angry ones or the super fans.

But that middle majority? The folks who had a decent experience and would totally recommend you?

They stay quiet... unless you invite them to speak up.

Feedback Helps You Grow

Reviews Help You Sell

There are really two sides to this coin:

1. **Feedback** helps you improve what's not working.
   It shows you where your process is clunky, your messaging is unclear, or your product needs tightening.

2. **Reviews** help future customers trust you.
   It's social proof. Credibility. Real people saying, "Yes, this was worth it."

You need both.

We Didn't Ask for Reviews Early On, And It Cost Us

Back when Frank launched one of his earlier digital products, he had a solid group of buyers, but his sales page looked... empty.

No testimonials. No feedback quotes. No credibility anchors. Why? Because he never asked.

When he finally started following up with customers, even just saying, "Hey, mind sharing a few thoughts about your experience?", the responses were gold.

Some turned into killer testimonials. Others gave him ideas to improve the product. And all of it helped future customers feel more confident saying yes.

Your Action Step

If you're not already doing this, start small:

- Send a quick post-purchase email 7–10 days after the sale.
- Ask: "How's it going? Anything you'd change?"
- Or: "Would you mind sharing a short review or testimonial I could use?"
- Make it easy, a link to a Google form, or even a reply-by-email works.

And don't be afraid to follow up. Sometimes people are happy to help, they just get busy. A gentle nudge can go a long way.

Bottom line?

Feedback helps you fix what's broken. Reviews help you sell what's working. Both come from the same place: asking.

So don't be afraid to ask. The answers might be exactly what your business needs to grow.

Chapter 59: Not Offering a Refund or Having a Shady Return Policy

Let's not beat around the bush…

> If your refund policy is vague, hidden, or
> worse, nonexistent, you're sending one
> message loud and clear:

"We don't stand behind what we sell."

That might not be your *intention*, but that's how it feels to a customer. And when people feel trapped? They walk away before they even buy.

Trust Makes the Sale, Not Pressure

We get it. You don't *want* people to refund. Nobody does. But refusing to offer a refund, or making it ridiculously hard to get one, doesn't reduce refunds.

It reduces **sales**.

Because customers get this weird sixth sense. If the policy feels sketchy, they hesitate. If it feels fair, clear, and respectful, they're more likely to buy in the first place.

A good refund policy doesn't hurt your business. It helps close more sales.

It says, "We believe in this enough to back it up."

A Shady Policy Does More Harm Than Good

Here's what a shady return policy might look like:

- Burying the terms in fine print
- Requiring people to "prove" they used the product
- Only accepting refunds during a random 72-hour window
- Making people jump through hoops just to get a response

Even if you *technically* have a policy... if it feels manipulative, you're losing goodwill, and probably getting refund requests **plus** a negative review.

Real Talk From Experience

One of the best moves we both made early on was offering a no-questions-asked 30-day money-back guarantee.

Yes, a few people took advantage of it. But the *increase* in conversions from people who felt safe buying far outweighed the handful who refunded.

And you know what else? We learned a ton from those refunds. Some gave honest feedback that was used to make the product better.

Others came back later and bought again, because they remembered how fairly they were treated the first time.

Your Action Step

Take a fresh look at your refund or return policy, on your sales pages, product checkout, and emails.

Ask yourself:

- Is it easy to find?
- Is it worded like a human would write it? Does it sound like you're trying to help... or trying to trap?

Make it clear. Make it generous (within reason). And most importantly, **make it honest.**

Because people don't expect perfection. They just want to know you're not going to vanish if things go sideways.

Bottom line?

A clear, fair refund policy builds trust. A shady one breaks it, sometimes before you even make the sale.

So put your integrity front and center. Stand behind what you sell. And your customers will stand behind you.

P.S. Be sure to check out the "Refund Policy Trust Builder" in your members area.

Chapter 60: Not Having a Community or Way to Engage Further

You made the sale. You delivered the product. You even followed up.

But then... radio silence.

No next step. No continued connection. No way for your customers to stay plugged in, ask questions, or feel like they're part of something bigger.

And that's a huge missed opportunity.

> Because in today's world, people aren't just looking for products, they're looking for connection.

They want to belong. To engage. To feel like they're part of a tribe, not just a transaction.

A Product Solves a Problem, But a Community Builds a Movement

Here's the thing:

People may come for the product, but they *stay* for the community.

Whether it's a private Facebook group, a members-only area, a Discord server, or even a simple monthly Zoom call, you need to give people a place to go once the transaction is over.

Because when do people feel connected to your brand *and* to each other? They stick around. They buy again. They refer to friends. They become your best marketers without you even asking.

"Your Network is your Net Worth"

- *Porter Gale*

We've Seen It Over and Over

Every time either of us has built some kind of community or open line of engagement, even if it's just a casual group or a follow-up thread, the relationship deepened.

People would ask more questions. They'd share results. They'd *talk to each other*, which meant less support strain.

And the biggest win? They felt like they were part of something. That kind of emotional connection isn't just feel-good fluff, it drives revenue. Loyalty. Longevity.

It Doesn't Have to Be Complicated

You don't need to spin up a giant forum or hire a full-time community manager.

Start simple:

- A private Facebook group for buyers.
- A welcome email that invites them to reply with their goals.
- A link to join a Slack channel or group thread.
- A short video or message that says, "Here's how to stay connected with us".
- Even just sending a check-in email 30 days later asking, "How are things going?"

It's not about *scale*. It's about **intentionality**.

Make it easy for people to stay in the loop, and feel like they matter beyond the checkout page.

Your Action Step

Ask yourself:

- After someone buys from me… then what?
- Is there a place they can go to get help, share wins, or connect with others?
- Am I making it *easy* for people to stay engaged?

If not, don't wait. Start small. Start scrappy. But **start**, because community isn't just a value-add.

It's a value-multiplier.

Bottom line?

If your customers feel like the door closes after the sale, they'll walk away.

But if you open the door to connection, conversation, and community? They'll walk through it, and stick around for the long haul.

Don't just build a customer list. Build a culture.

Scaling & Operations Mistakes

So, you've got a business that's up and running. You're making sales. You've got happy customers. Things are moving.

But here's where many online entrepreneurs hit the wall:

> They get stuck *working in* the business instead of building a system that grows *beyond* them.

Because scaling isn't just about doing more of what works.
It's about creating **repeatable systems, smarter operations, and strategic leverage** that frees up your time while growing your impact.

In this section, we're shifting gears from front-end experience to back-end efficiency.

We'll dig into the overlooked mistakes that stop good businesses from scaling, and show you how to avoid becoming the bottleneck in your own success.

Let's get to it. Your next level starts here.

Chapter 61: Not Legally Structuring the Business (LLC, S-Corp, etc.)

Let's get real for a second…

> If you're running an online business without *any* legal structure in place, you're not just risking your profits, you're risking everything.

Your personal assets. Your tax situation. Even your credibility.

Now, I'm not a lawyer and I'm not giving you legal advice here. But we are telling you, **this is one mistake that can quietly cost you big time down the road.**

Starting as a "Sole Proprietor" Is Fine… for a Minute

A lot of online entrepreneurs start out solo, selling a product, building a site, maybe freelancing.

And that's totally fine.

But as soon as money starts moving, things get real. Because without a legal structure, there's **no line** between your business and your personal life.

- Get sued? Your bank account's fair game.
- Need funding? Good luck.
- Looking to sell the business someday? Not going to happen without structure.

What Structure Makes Sense?

There's no one-size-fits-all answer, but here are the common ones:

- **Sole Proprietor** – Easiest to start, but offers zero legal protection.

- **LLC (Limited Liability Company)** – Great middle ground. Simple to form. Protects your personal assets.

- **S-Corp** – More complex, but can offer real tax advantages if your business income is growing.

- **C-Corp** – Mostly for larger companies with shareholders. Overkill for most solo entrepreneurs.

Again, talk to a CPA or business attorney to make the right call. But whatever you do, **don't ignore it.**

Your Business Isn't a Hobby Anymore

Here's what we see too often:

People run their online business like it's "just a side hustle." They figure, "I'll deal with all that legal stuff later."

Then later becomes too late.

They land a big client who wants a W-9… and realize they're not set up. Or they get audited… and can't separate personal and business income. Or they want to scale… but nobody takes them seriously because their biz isn't official.

> **If you want to grow, you have to act like a real business.**

And part of that is getting the structure right.

Your Action Step

If you haven't yet:

1. Talk to a qualified accountant or attorney about the best structure for *your* situation.

2. Choose a legal entity (LLC is often a great first step).
3. Get a separate business bank account.
4. Start keeping clean records, separate from your personal finances.

You don't have to know it all. You just have to **start the process.**

Be sure to claim your free bonus report "The Costly Mistake of Ignoring Business Structure" from our good friend and wealth attorney JJ Childers.

👉 Visit 50BiggestOnlineBusinessMistakes.com/bookbonus

Bottom line?

You can't scale what you haven't protected. So take the time. Do the paperwork. Get legit.

It's not just about taxes or liability, it's about *treating your business like it matters*. Because it does.

Chapter 62: No Documented Systems or SOPs

Let us guess…

You've got a dozen things you do every week in your business. You know them inside and out. You're fast. You're efficient. It works.

Until one day… you get busy. Or sick. Or you want to hire help. And suddenly, all that "stuff in your head" becomes a bottleneck.

> Because if everything lives in your brain, your business is one skipped step away from chaos.

That's where SOPs come in, **Standard Operating Procedures.**

Now before you roll your eyes or zone out, let me make this super clear:

> **This isn't about writing a manual the size of a phone book.**

It's about building freedom.

Systems = Scale

If you ever want to...

- Take a vacation
- Hire a VA or team member
- Work *on* the business instead of *in* it
- Sell your company someday

...you need documented systems.

They don't have to be fancy. They just have to be *repeatable.*

Because systems create consistency. Consistency creates reliability. And reliability builds business people's trust.

We Learned the Hard Way

Back in the early days, Frank had a VA helping him with customer support. She was great... until she wasn't available one week, and Frank had to jump in.

He realized he hadn't documented *anything.*

How they handled logins. How they replied to certain questions. Where they stored order receipts. What to do when someone wants a refund.

It was all stuff he knew, but nobody else did. And that was on him.

So he started writing things down. Recording screens. Making simple checklists. Not because he wanted to create bureaucracy, but because he wanted **peace of mind.**

SOPs Don't Need to Be Complicated

You can start small:

- A Google Doc with step-by-step instructions.
- A checklist inside a project management tool.
- A 3-minute Loom video walking through a task.
- A folder called "How We Do Things" that your team can use.

The point is... once it's documented, it's off your plate. And someone else can take it over with confidence.

Your Action Step

Pick **one** task you do more than once a week.

Write it down like you're handing it to a brand-new assistant.

- What's the first step?
- What needs to be double-checked?
- What's the finished outcome supposed to look like?

That's your first SOP.

Build one a week, and in a couple months, you'll have a business that runs smoother, and grows faster, because it's not all depending on your memory.

Bottom line?

If your business only works when *you* do, you don't own a business, you own a job.

Start documenting. Start delegating. And start building a business that can thrive without you pulling every lever.

P.S. Check out the sample "Simple SOP Starter Template" In the members area.

Chapter 63: Ignoring Bookkeeping, Taxes, or Legal Protection

Look, we get it. When you're deep in the hustle of building your online business, it's easy to focus on the fun stuff:

Launching products. Building websites. Getting that next sale.

But there's a whole other side of business that doesn't feel as exciting until you realize ignoring it can blow a giant hole in everything you've worked for.

> We're talking about your **bookkeeping, taxes, and legal protection.**

Unsexy? Sure. Essential? Absolutely.

If You Don't Track It, You Can't Grow It

Let's start with bookkeeping.

This isn't just about "being organized." It's about:

- Knowing what you're spending
- Seeing which products make money
- Planning for slow seasons or unexpected expenses

- Making smarter decisions based on real data, not gut feelings

If you're just guessing… you're gambling.

And if tax time rolls around and your numbers are a mess?
You'll either overpay, underpay (and risk penalties), or spend days scrambling through receipts you forgot to categorize.

What you don't track can cost you.

The IRS Doesn't Care That You're "Just Online"

A lot of online entrepreneurs assume that because they don't have a storefront, they're flying under the radar.

But trust me, **digital doesn't mean invisible.**

Your payment processor, your ad platform, and even your bank reports activity. And if you're not setting aside money for taxes, or worse, not filing at all, you're asking for trouble.

We've seen people get hit with multi-year tax bills *plus* penalties and interest because they didn't take it seriously.

Don't let that be you.

Legal Protection Isn't Just for Big Businesses

You might think, *"I'm just a one-person shop. Nobody's going to sue me."*

Until they do.

It could be:

- A client dispute.
- A copyright claim.
- A refund gone sideways.
- Someone misusing your product and trying to blame you for it.

If you don't have the right disclaimers, contracts, or policies in place, **you're exposed.**

And that exposure could mean losing not just your business, but your personal savings, your home, everything.

We Didn't Love This Stuff Either Until It Was a Savior

Years ago, Frank had a dispute over some website work. He thought he was covered. Turns out, he didn't have a written contract in place.

What should've been a simple conversation turned into a legal mess. It cost him more than it should've, all because he didn't want to "deal with the boring stuff."

Now? He treats those "boring" parts of the business-like *insurance for success.*

They're not what gets the spotlight... but they're what keep the spotlight from burning your whole stage down.

Your Action Step

Let's simplify this:

- If you don't have a bookkeeper or accounting system, get one. Even if it's just QuickBooks, Wave, or a Google Sheet for now.

- Set aside 25–30% of your income for taxes (and talk to a CPA, you'll thank yourself).

- Review your contracts, terms, and policies. Get a legit agreement template for client work or digital product disclaimers.

- And if your business is growing, talk to a business attorney **before** you need one.

This stuff isn't just about staying out of trouble. It's about running a *real* business.

Bottom line?

Ignoring the financial and legal side of your business doesn't make it go away. It just makes the consequences hit harder when they show up.

So get your foundation in order. Track your money. Protect your work. Pay your taxes. Your future self, and your business, will thank you.

Chapter 64: Not Reinvesting Profits Into Growth

Let's talk about something a lot of new business owners get wrong:

They finally start making money... and immediately start spending it, on the wrong things.

New gear. Fancy software they don't need yet. A "reward" vacation.

Now, don't get us wrong. You *should* celebrate your wins. That's part of what keeps you motivated.

But if you're pulling all your profits out of the business without putting anything back in? You're starving the very thing that got you here in the first place.

A Business Isn't a Piggy Bank

You didn't build your business to live invoice to invoice. You built it to create something sustainable, scalable, and *stable.*

But here's the catch: that doesn't happen by accident. It takes **investment.**

That could mean:

- Hiring your first contractor to take repetitive tasks off your plate.

- Upgrading tools that will actually save time or improve customer experience.

- Putting money into ads, training, or systems that bring a measurable return.

- Rebranding or redesigning your site to better match the level you've reached.

Every dollar you reinvest wisely is a step closer to long-term freedom.

We Had to Learn This the Hard Way

When we started making real money online, we thought we'd made it. Computers were upgraded. New gadgets were purchased. A few "just because" trips were taken.

And then a dry spell hit. Sales slowed down. Leads were needed. Help was needed. Momentum was needed.

But no money had been reinvested, money had only been *spent.*

The business wasn't building. It was draining.

That was the turning point. A percentage of profits began being budgeted every month specifically for business growth.

And guess what? The next time things dipped, the systems, leads, and support were in place to bounce back fast.

Reinvestment Isn't Just Smart, It's Strategic

Want to scale? Want to stop being the bottleneck? Then you need to start thinking like a CEO, not a freelancer.

Reinvestment shows up in the form of:

- **Tools** that save time
- **People** who help you execute
- **Marketing** that brings in traffic
- **Training** that sharpens your skills
- **Assets** that keep working when you're offline

You don't need to dump every dollar back in. But setting aside even 10–30% of profits for growth can change everything.

Your Action Step

This week, ask yourself:

- What's the one area of my business that's holding me back from the next level?
- Is it time? Leads? Skill? Delivery?
- What's one investment I could make *right now* that would move the needle in that area?

Then commit to a reinvestment habit. Even small steps, taken consistently, turn into big momentum.

Bottom line?

The money you make today should help you create more money tomorrow. So don't just celebrate your wins. Leverage them.

Feed the machine that funds your freedom.

P.S. There's a valuable "Reinvestment Planner Worksheet" inside your members area.

Chapter 65: Waiting Too Long to Pivot When Something Isn't Working

Let's have a heart-to-heart.

> One of the most expensive mistakes in business isn't making the *wrong* move, it's **staying stuck in the wrong move, for too long.**

You launch a product that flops. You invest in a strategy that doesn't convert. You double down on an offer that used to work… but doesn't anymore.

Instead of adjusting, you wait. You hope. You tell yourself, "Maybe next month."

And before you know it? You've wasted time, money, energy, and sometimes confidence, because you didn't pivot when the writing was already on the wall.

Loyalty to a Broken System Doesn't Make You Smart, It Makes You Stalled

We've seen it with online courses that barely sell but the creator keeps tweaking the *sales page* instead of the offer.

We've seen people stuck with the wrong niche, clinging to a podcast or brand because they already put so much time into it, even though it's not growing.

Heck, we've done it ourselves.

> Because it's easier to stay the course than admit the course needs to change.

But success doesn't come from being stubborn. It comes from **being willing to adapt. Quickly.**

Business Is a Series of Adjustments

There's no perfect path. You test. You learn. You adjust. You move forward.

Sometimes a pivot is minor, like changing a headline or switching your email strategy. Sometimes it's major, like retiring a product or shifting your whole business model.

But either way, the worst thing you can do is ignore the signs and *hope* things improve. Hope is not a strategy.

We've Pivoted Multiple Times

There are products we loved that no longer fit our audience. Funnels were built that didn't convert. Ideas we thought were brilliant... that just didn't land.

But every time the call was made to pivot, sooner rather than later, it freed up space to build what actually worked.

You're not failing when you pivot. You're learning. You're evolving. You're protecting your momentum.

And momentum is everything in business.

Your Action Step

Look at your current efforts:

- What's not working *right now* that you've been avoiding dealing with?

- Is there a product, process, or platform that's become a time or money pit? Are you still investing in something that's not producing a return?

Then ask yourself: *Am I staying the course out of strategy... or out of fear to change?*

If it's the latter, it's time to pivot.

Start with one small step, kill the dead weight, reframe the message, test a new angle.

Just move.

Bottom line?

The ability to pivot quickly isn't just a skill, it's a survival strategy. Don't let pride or sunk cost hold your business hostage.

Make decisions based on data, not emotion. Adjust early. Adjust often. And keep moving forward.

P.S. A "Pivot Trigger Checklist" is available for you in the members area.

Chapter 66: Trying to Do Everything Yourself (No Delegation or Automation)

Let's be honest…

You might be the boss, but if you're doing *everything* yourself, you're not running a business… you're Wearing a straightjacket.

We get it. Nobody can do it quite like you. You know your tools, your customers, your flow. You built it from scratch, this is *your* baby.

But if your business can't run without you pushing every button? You don't have a scalable company. You've got a stressful job.

"You can do anything, but not everything."

– David Allen

You Can't Scale While You're Drowning in To-Dos

- Designing the graphics
- Writing the emails
- Answering the support tickets
- Posting to social media
- Processing payments
- Building the sales page
- Updating the plugins

Sound familiar? It's noble at first. Even necessary. But eventually it becomes the bottleneck that stalls growth and steals your sanity.

> **If everything depends on you, everything will eventually stop with you.**

Delegation Isn't a Luxury, It's a Growth Strategy

Most solopreneurs think, *"I'll hire help when I can afford it."*

But often, **you can't afford to keep doing it all yourself.**

Hiring a VA for just 5–10 hours a week can free up hours of your time.

Time you can use to:

- Focus on higher-level strategy
- Serve more clients
- Create new offers
- Or simply… rest (crazy idea, I know)

Delegation isn't about dumping tasks. It's about freeing your energy so you can focus on what *actually* grows your business.

And Then There's Automation

You don't need a team of 10 when you've got the right tools doing work in the background.

- Email sequences
- Cart abandonment follow-ups
- Onboarding workflows
- Calendar bookings
- Social post scheduling

These aren't "nice to haves", they're **efficiency machines** that run while you sleep. Set them up once, and let them do the heavy lifting on autopilot.

Frank Had to Let Go to Level Up

For years, Frank wore every hat. Tech. Design. Support. Delivery. And he took pride in it, until he realized he was working more hours *as a business owner* than he did when he had a job.

So he started with one task. Then another. Then he found a few tools that saved hours every week. That's when things really took off.

Because now, he could focus on the work that moved the needle, not just the work that filled his calendar.

Your Action Step

Here's a quick exercise:

Make a list of every recurring task you do each week. Then ask:

- Does *this* need to be done by me?
- Could I train someone else to do it?
- Could a tool or system automate it?

Start by offloading just *one* thing, then another.

Before you know it, your days will feel lighter, your focus will sharpen, and your business will finally have room to grow.

Bottom line?

You can be the visionary, or you can be the bottleneck. But you can't be both. Let go of control, invest in support, and build systems that scale.

Because success isn't just about working hard... it's about learning when to **stop doing it all yourself.**

Epilogue: This Isn't the End, It's Just the Beginning

So here we are, Chapter 66 in the rearview mirror, 50+ of the biggest online business mistakes now exposed and (hopefully) on your radar.

And if you've made it all the way through, let us just say:
Well done.

Most people *don't* take the time to study the potholes before speeding down the road.

But you did.

That tells us something important:

You're not just dabbling. You're not just "hoping this works." You're building something that matters, and you want to do it *right*.

We've shared a lot with you in these pages.

Some of it was strategic. Some were technical. Some were mindset-related. And all of it came from real-world experience, ours, and those we've worked with over the years.

We didn't write this book because it sounded like a good idea.

We wrote it because we're tired of seeing great people with great ideas struggle, stall out, or quit altogether, simply because they didn't see the mistakes coming.

And now? **You do.**

The Real Test Starts Now

Reading this book is only the first move.

The next is putting it into practice.

That doesn't mean trying to fix everything at once (please don't). It means taking *one* chapter that hit you hardest and asking:

"What would change if I fixed just this one thing?"

Start there. Fix that. Then move on to the next.

Each small shift creates momentum. And momentum creates progress. And progress… is how businesses are built.

You Don't Have to Do This Alone

We know this book was packed, with 66 chapters worth of tough lessons, honest truths, and actionable takeaways.

That's why we created a special companion resource page just for readers like you.

Visit 50BiggestOnlineBusinessMistakes.com/bookbonus

Inside, you'll find:

- Downloadable tools, checklists, and templates.
- Bonus training we couldn't fit in the book.
- Worksheets to help you apply what you've learned.
- Updates as the online business world continues to shift.
- And a few surprises just for action-takers.

You'll also find ways to connect with us, ask questions, and continue the journey.

Because this isn't the end of our conversation, it's just the beginning.

Final Thought

If there's one thing we hope you walk away with, it's this:

Mistakes don't mean failure. They mean you're in the game.

And now, you've got the playbook to keep moving forward with clarity, confidence, and control.

So go build something you're proud of. Fix what's broken.
Skip the struggle. And finally...

Build a business that works.

We'll see you on the road to success.

Frank Deardurff III & Bret Ridgway

One Last Favor...

If this book helped you, even in just one small but meaningful way, we'd be incredibly grateful if you'd **recommend it to a fellow entrepreneur** who might be facing similar struggles.

And if you have a moment, a quick review on Amazon or Goodreads goes a long way in helping us reach others who are stuck and searching for answers, just like you were.

Thanks again for letting us be part of your journey. We can't wait to see what you build next.

Resources Mentioned in the Book

These are tools, services, and references mentioned throughout the chapters to help you streamline, automate, and grow your online business.

Tools & Platforms

- **WordPress.org** – Build your own website with complete control.
- **Google Analytics** – Track visitor behavior and site performance.
- **Google Search Console** – Monitor SEO performance and indexing issues.
- **QuickBooks / Wave Accounting** – For managing bookkeeping and tracking finances.
- **Zoom** – For live meetings, webinars, and client calls.
- **Loom** – Record screen-share walkthroughs for training or SOPs.
- **Trello / Asana / ClickUp** – Project and task management systems.
- **Canva** – Easy drag-and-drop graphics and content creation.
- **MailerLite / ConvertKit / ActiveCampaign / Aweber / Flodesk** – Email marketing platforms.
- **Facebook Groups / Discord / Circle.so** – Tools to build community.

- **Calendly** – Automate meeting bookings with clients or leads.
- **Stripe / PayPal** – Secure online payment processing.
- **LastPass / 1Password** – Store and manage secure login credentials.

Business & Legal Resources

- **Score.org** - America's largest network of volunteer business mentors providing free guidance and resources to help small businesses succeed.
- **LegalZoom / Rocket Lawyer** – Affordable legal formation help (LLC, S-Corp, etc.).
- **IRS.gov** – U.S. federal tax guidance and forms.
- **TermsFeed / Termly** – Create privacy policies, disclaimers, and terms of service.
- **Upwork / Fiverr** – Hire freelancers for design, tech, writing, etc.
- **OnlineBusinessManager.com** – Source OBMs and virtual team help.

Templates & Downloads

Available at

50BiggestOnlineBusinessMistakes.com/bookbonus

- "What to Fix First" Quick Start Guide.
- Simple SOP Starter Template.
- Relationship Builder Touchpoint Map.
- Refund Policy Trust Builder Template.
- Delegate & Automate Task Tracker.
- Pivot Trigger Checklist.
- Reinvestment Planner Worksheet.
- The Costly Mistake of Ignoring Business Structure

Glossary of Common Online Business Terms

A handy reference if you need a refresher on the language of the digital business world. New to the online business world? Bookmark this glossary. These are the terms we reference throughout the book, and the ones you'll hear often in your entrepreneurial journey.

A/B Testing – Comparing two versions of a web page, email, or ad to see which performs better.

ADA (Americans with Disabilities Act) – U.S. legislation that requires businesses, including websites, to be accessible to people with disabilities. For online businesses, this means ensuring your site can be used by individuals with visual, auditory, or motor impairments, using tools like alt text for images, keyboard navigation, readable fonts, and proper color contrast. Non-compliance can lead to legal risk and lost sales opportunities.

Affiliate Marketing – A marketing strategy where others promote your product and earn a commission for each sale they generate.

Autoresponder – A series of pre-written emails automatically sent to subscribers after they opt in, often used for onboarding or lead nurturing.

Bounce Rate – The percentage of visitors who leave your website after viewing only one page.

Call-to-Action (CTA) – A prompt encouraging the user to take a specific action (e.g., "Buy Now," "Sign Up Today").

CAN-SPAM Act – U.S. legislation that sets rules for commercial email, including rules around unsubscribe links and sender identity.

Click-Through Rate (CTR) – The percentage of people who click a link or button after seeing it in an ad, email, or on a web page.

Conversion Rate – The percentage of visitors who take a desired action (buy, opt-in, etc.).

Cookie Policy – A legal notice that explains how your website uses cookies (small data files stored on a visitor's device) to track activity, personalize content, or analyze traffic. Required in many countries (especially under laws like GDPR), a cookie policy helps ensure transparency and builds trust with site visitors. Many sites also include a pop-up or banner asking users to accept cookies upon visiting.

Copywriting – Writing persuasive content (sales pages, emails, ads) designed to get readers to take a specific action.

CRM (Customer Relationship Management) – A system to manage customer data, sales pipelines, and communication.

DNS (Domain Name System) – The system that connects your domain name (like yourwebsite.com) to your hosting server so people can access your site.

Email List – A collection of email addresses gathered from leads or customers for future marketing.

Evergreen Content – Content that stays relevant and valuable over time (as opposed to time-sensitive promotions).

Funnel – A series of steps designed to guide a visitor toward a conversion or sale.

Freemium – A pricing model that offers a basic version of a product or service for free, with paid upgrades for premium features.

GDPR (General Data Protection Regulation) – A European data privacy law that affects how businesses collect, store, and use personal data.

Heatmap – A visual tool that shows how visitors interact with your web page, where they click, scroll, and linger.

Hosting – A service that stores your website's files and makes them accessible online.

Landing Page – A standalone web page designed specifically to convert visitors into leads or customers.

Lead Magnet – A free resource offered in exchange for a prospect's contact information.

Open Rate – The percentage of email recipients who open a specific email campaign.

Opt-In – When a user agrees to receive emails or content, often in exchange for a freebie.

Payment Gateway – A service (like Stripe or PayPal) that securely processes customer payments on your website.

Pixel – A small piece of code (like the Facebook Pixel) used to track user behavior for ads or analytics.

Privacy Policy – A legal document that discloses what personal information your site collects and how it's used.

Reciprocal Promotion – An agreement where two business owners promote each other's products to their own audiences.

Retargeting / Remarketing – Showing ads to people who've visited your site or interacted with your content but haven't converted yet.

ROI (Return on Investment) – A measurement of the profitability of a marketing effort or business investment.

Scarcity – A psychological trigger used in marketing that emphasizes limited availability to create urgency.

Split Testing – Another term for A/B testing, used to compare performance of two different versions of a marketing element.

SOP (Standard Operating Procedure) – A documented step-by-step guide to performing a task consistently.

SSL (Secure Socket Layer) – A security protocol that encrypts data between your site and visitors (HTTPS).

Terms of Service (ToS) – A set of rules and guidelines users must agree to when using your website or purchasing from you.

Upsell / Downsell – Additional offers made during or after a purchase to increase transaction value.

UX (User Experience) – The overall experience a person has when interacting with your website or product.

V.A. (Virtual Assistant) – A remote worker who helps with admin, tech, or marketing tasks.

Webinar – A live or recorded online presentation used to educate, engage, and often sell to a targeted audience.

About The Authors

About Frank Deardurff
That One Web Guy

Frank Deardurff, also known as That One Web Guy, is a veteran of the online business world with nearly 30 years of experience helping entrepreneurs turn digital chaos into clarity.

He's not just a tech troubleshooter, he's a trusted business strategist, seasoned coach, dynamic trainer, and skilled graphic artist who understands both the design and performance sides of online marketing.

Over the years, Frank has worked behind the scenes with some of the biggest names in the industry, helping them clean up broken websites, fix underperforming funnels, streamline their processes, and finally get the results they were chasing.

Whether he's coding, coaching, or creating Frank's mission is the same:

To help you stop spinning your wheels and start building a business that works.

To find out more and connect with Frank visit: ThatOneWebGuy.com

About Bret Ridgway

The No-Hype Business Voice

With over 25 years of behind-the-scenes experience in online marketing, Bret Ridgway has seen what works—and what doesn't—at every level of the industry.

As the co-founder of Speaker Fulfillment Services, he's supported hundreds of top speakers, authors, and information marketers with product creation, order fulfillment, and event logistics. His unique vantage point has given him a front-row seat to the real business strategies that drive lasting success—not just flashy launches or surface-level hype.

Bret is also a multiple-time author, a trusted voice in product marketing circles, and the host of the long-running podcast, Spotlight on Speaking, where he helps speakers and thought leaders grow their influence and income.

Known for his calm, practical, no-BS approach, Bret brings clarity and grounded wisdom to entrepreneurs who are serious about building sustainable success without falling for the next shiny object.

If you're tired of the noise, Bret's the guy you want in your corner.

If you'd like to discover what's going on in Bret's world, Visit either BretRidgway.com or SpotlightOnSpeaking.com

Together, Bret and Frank bring you hard-won wisdom and practical fixes you won't get from theory-driven marketing books.